OUR PRISTINE MIND

Our
PRISTINE
MIND

A PRACTICAL GUIDE TO
UNCONDITIONAL
HAPPINESS

Orgyen Chowang

SHAMBHALA
BOULDER
2016

Shambhala Publications, Inc.
4720 Walnut Street
Boulder, Colorado 80301
www.shambhala.com

Author photo by Stephanie Mohan
Pristine Mind® is a registered trademark of Pristine Mind Foundation.

9 8 7 6 5 4 3 2 1

First Edition
Printed in the United States of America

∞ This edition is printed on acid-free paper that meets the
American National Standards Institute Z39.48 Standard.
♻ This book is printed on 30% postconsumer recycled paper.
For more information please visit www.shambhala.com.

Distributed in the United States by Penguin Random House LLC and in
Canada by Random House of Canada Ltd

Designed by Gopa & Ted2, Inc.

Library of Congress Cataloging-in-Publication Data

Chowang, Orgyen, author.
Our pristine mind: a practical guide to unconditional happiness /
Orgyen Chowang.—First edition.
pages cm
ISBN 978-1-61180-327-3 (paperback)
1. Meditation. 2. Meditation—Buddhism. 3. Spiritual life.
4. Mind and body. 5. Happiness. I. Title.
BL627.C563 2016
294.3'444—dc23
2015027659

This book is dedicated and offered to my
enlightened master, Jigme Phuntsok Rinpoche,
who brought meaning, purpose, and happiness to my life.

Contents

PREFACE

O UR *PRISTINE MIND* is a practical guide to unconditional happiness. Experiencing our Pristine Mind—who we really are—and thereby achieving true, unconditional happiness, is what this book is about. To introduce this profound, transformative path of experience to you, I would like to tell you first how this book came to exist. I hope that sharing my own journey with you will give you a deeper understanding of the journey you are about to undertake.

I spent my childhood in Eastern Tibet, in a small village. Oftentimes I found myself in the hills above the village, just gazing at the clear blue sky and the clouds passing by. I enjoyed that peaceful time, with my mind spacious and clear like the sky above.

At the age of fourteen I received the rare opportunity to become a student of one of the greatest enlightened masters of the twentieth century, Jigme Phuntsok Rinpoche. I left home and started my studies at Larung Gar, my teacher's famous retreat center. The living conditions at Larung Gar at that time were harsh, with very cold winters, scanty food, and few comforts. For the first year I lived on my uncle's porch, with only a curtain protecting me from the snow. After that, my parents built me a small house, where I stayed for the next eight years of my training. Even though the living conditions continued to be challenging, they never felt too difficult to bear. In fact, this was a time in my life when I experienced tremendous joy.

During these nine years, my focus was on studying the canon of Buddhist literature, particularly the advanced teachings known in Tibet as Vajrayana and Dzogchen. But my studies were not just dry reading and test taking, as you might imagine. I found great inspiration and joy through singing "vajra songs"—poems that have arisen in the minds of enlightened masters out of their meditation experiences. These poems express extraordinary wisdom. After each day of class and study, I went back to my little house and sang many vajra songs, particularly those of the great masters Longchenpa (fourteenth century) and Mipham Rinpoche (nineteenth century).

After many years of study, I was given the title Khenpo, the rough equivalent of a Ph.D. It indicates having a full understanding of the Buddhist literature and also means having achieved some degree of meditation experience, so that I was qualified to give teachings and guide others in their practice as well. Overall, the training I received during these years gave me the knowledge and practical tools I needed in order to lead a life of fulfillment and transformation, for both myself and others. I embarked on a career in teaching. I was especially attracted to the idea of traveling and teaching in many places around the world.

A few years later I met Thinley Norbu Rinpoche, an extraordinary and highly esteemed teacher and author. We made a close connection, and I received teachings from him. In late 1995 he invited me to visit him in the United States. I spent about four months at his residence in upstate New York. Then I moved to Santa Cruz, California, to teach at the great yogi Lama Tharchin Rinpoche's dharma center. When I first came to the United States, I only knew a few words of English, like "hello" and "goodbye." Still, I was fascinated with meeting people and finding out about how they lived and how they viewed the world.

I ended up staying at Lama Tharchin's center for three years. It was an exciting and interesting experience. I gave teachings at a *shedra,* or college of Buddhist studies, which ran for about a month every year, and I also gave informal teachings to students who lived there or visited from time to time. Some very good interpreters were provided to translate into English as I spoke Tibetan. During this time I learned more and more about how people speak and understand English.

The translators were very skilled. But despite their abilities, I didn't feel satisfied that the students were really "getting" what I was teaching. It wasn't the translators' fault. The problem was really the way language works. For your listeners to get the true experience of what you teach, you need to have your own "voice"—you need to select your own words and phrases, and not have someone else choose the words for you. No matter how good your translator is, if you don't personally choose your own words so as to say what you really mean, the translation will distort the meaning to some degree, and the meaning won't be received by the listeners in a clear and powerful way. So I thought a lot about how to deal with this problem.

In 1999 I moved to the San Francisco Bay Area. While living there, I gathered with students in the Napa Valley four times a year and taught meditation with an excellent translator. As I listened to people's questions and my translator's way of expressing my thoughts, I understood the English language more and more and realized how powerful it could be in conveying the teachings; but also I knew more and more that the full message of what I was trying to communicate wasn't really getting across. I needed to speak more directly with people and develop my own spiritual language in English.

So for the next few years, except for the Napa Valley retreats, I kept mostly to myself. Working with only one person, Josh Godine, as my assistant, I began writing a book. I still didn't speak English very well, yet I started to write a book in English! It was crazy, but I was determined. I told Josh that by publishing a book we could achieve two valuable goals: we could develop a very natural, experiential language for clearly expressing the teachings of meditation and, even more important, we could share these teachings effectively with others.

During this time, while I worked on that book, mostly I simply lived quietly at home, practicing meditation and deepening my meditation experience. Sometimes I went out to coffee shops and other public places to see how people spent their time. I watched TV news—not so much for the news, but to improve my English and observe how people perceive themselves and the world. I spent some time with a few students. I pored over the texts I had studied during my training. I sang vajra songs.

Slowly, Josh and I compiled transcripts of talks I had given about different types of meditation into a manuscript that I titled "Power of Meditation." It was informative, yet it still contained vocabulary that made it only understandable to readers who were already familiar with these types of teachings. I knew that readers who were unfamiliar with the subject matter would find the book hard to follow.

After working on that manuscript for some time, I began to realize that there was something more that I needed to say, and that I had to say it in a more direct way. I had the aspiration to write a guide to the entire path of meditation in one book, from the moment the reader begins this journey, up to the time of becoming an advanced meditator, and gradually all the way to complete enlightenment.

With this inspiration, I put that first manuscript aside and began to work on a new book. That was the beginning of *Our Pristine Mind*.

A personal turning point for me occurred between 2004, the time I first began work on this book, and 2008. Previously, with all my studies, I had understood the Buddha's teachings intellectually, but I did not feel my experiential insight was anywhere near as profound as it could be. But now, during these four years, I really concentrated on my own practice at the same time I was working on this book. I was striving to live by the principles of this book, and I was also eager to share these principles effectively with other people.

A tremendous help in unfolding the content of this book was the teaching I did during this time. At the Napa Valley retreats, I practiced meditation together with my students for periods ranging from three to five days. I gave oral teachings, both in Tibetan with my translator, and in English with the translator helping to put my broken English into standard English. All these teachings were recorded. The recordings were transcribed to create the material for this book. Then Josh and I edited the transcripts to make them clearer and more succinct. My facility with written English improved as I learned new words and looked for ways of expressing my meaning more precisely and more naturally, without academic or intellectual overlays.

The fruition of this time that I spent dedicated to my meditation practice and working on the book came in 2011. A beautifully descriptive term came to me: "Pristine Mind."

I was so excited and inspired to find the term "Pristine Mind"—more excited and inspired than I had ever been. Finding this term was like finding a home. It was a really amazing experience. I realized, "This is it! This communicates everything! Now I have a perfect name for giving Dzogchen teachings—Pristine Mind meditation. Now I have a name for my organization—Pristine Mind Foundation." Gaining that name was very important. It is very, very precious.

In the Dzogchen teachings, there is a Tibetan term, *ka dag,* short for *ka nay dag pa. Ka dag* means "pristine from the beginning." *Ka* is the first letter of the Tibetan alphabet, like the letter *A* in English. If something is pristine starting from *A*, that means it is completely, utterly pure and pristine—pristine from the beginning, or innately pristine.

Then there is also the term *ka dag rig pa*, which means "pristine mind" or "pristine awareness." So the meaning of the Dzogchen term *ka dag rig pa* is unlocked in English when it is translated as "Pristine Mind." You can practically touch or taste "Pristine Mind"—it feels cool, crisp, and refreshing, like pristine waters. Discovering that key was a really satisfying and delightful experience. Now the book could fully unfold.

Each time I meditated with students, I gave a "test drive" to Pristine Mind and the way it conveyed the meaning of the teachings. Each time we gathered together, the sense of the term became more clear and graspable than before. It is not just through conceptual understanding but also through meditation that the meaning has become clearer and clearer.

"Pristine Mind" is a genuine, unfabricated Dzogchen term. As I continued to work on the book and give teachings, other Dzogchen terms revealed themselves in natural, nonintellectual English. All of the special terms that I use in this book—*Pristine Mind, mental events, ordinary mind, undistorted perception,* and others—embody the traditional Dzogchen language and bring it to life in contemporary English.

But although I have carefully chosen the English words to embody these teachings, I must emphasize that the *source* of the teachings is the Buddha and the teachings of Guru Rinpoche Padmasambhava, who is called the Second Buddha for his role in bringing the teachings of the Buddha to Tibet. In addition, Longchenpa, Mipham Rinpoche, and my precious teacher, Jigme Phuntsok Rinpoche, are great masters whose teachings are crucial to this book. I relied completely on the wisdom of all these masters. The opportunity to express and communicate their teachings in the English language is a great privilege. My heart is filled with tremendous appreciation and gratitude for these enlightened teachers and their teachings. They have been, and will continue to be, the source of great benefit to myself and others.

Our Pristine Mind is that guide to the entire path that I longed to write for so many years. The teachings can be understood and mastered by everyone who practices them. After you have read this book and engaged in the practice, you will emerge with a very different understanding of your mind and your world than you had before.

The goal of Pristine Mind meditation—as well as my own wish for you—is to realize and experience Pristine Mind. Everybody possesses Pristine Mind, since it is our true nature; but we each need to uncover it for ourselves. Revealing Pristine Mind now and for future generations to come, and helping everyone to find unconditional happiness—that is the purpose of this book.

The teachings that were given to me, and that I now wish to pass on to you, I believe in and know to be true with all my heart. But you do not have to take my word for it, nor should you. Let the teachings speak to you directly, and make your own decision.

Our Pristine Mind

Introduction

OUR HUMAN LIFE is so precious, it seems we ought to be happy. We are taught that we can be happy if we work hard to achieve the goals we are told to strive for: looking young and attractive, having a good relationship, succeeding at work, and making good money, for example. When we think we are doing well in life, it's usually because we feel happy for the time being or we are satisfied, even delighted, with our positive circumstances. When we fall in love, buy the new car, or get the promotion we have worked so hard for, we experience high spirits. But sooner or later we learn that such happiness is short-lived or tainted with problems of one kind or another.

No matter how much happiness we get out of our circumstances, we eventually reach a point where we feel uncertain, stressed, and unhappy. We feel that if we just had a little more of this or a little less of that, or if we could just figure out what's lacking, then we would find true happiness. But reaching that elusive place is so rare. Our times of happiness turn to times of sadness. The things we had hoped would bring complete, perfect happiness simply fail to do so.

Clearly, something is missing. Even when we succeed in getting the things that are supposed to bring happiness, we do not feel fundamentally, unconditionally happy. By fundamental or unconditional happiness, I mean not merely temporary happiness but a contentment that is indestructible. It does not depend on any external causes or conditions or circumstances.

In truth, the problem is not with our possessions, our relationships, our status in life, or other circumstances. The problem is with our own mind.

That may sound pretty serious. What's wrong with our mind? How can we fix our mind? Fortunately, there *is* something we can do. It is not as difficult as you might think. In fact, there are only a few thoughts between you and happiness.

For many hundreds of years, the meditation masters of my lineage have experienced and taught an understanding of the human mind that fully answers the challenge of finding unconditional happiness. My teachers, and their teachers before them, preserved this understanding for posterity. But today, the traditional manner in which this wisdom has been presented does not speak to a large majority of people. It all sounds exotic, mystical, or foreign to them, with terms such as "enlightenment" defined in ways that remain puzzling.

It does not have to be such a mystery. The path to enlightenment is a straightforward, logical, realistic, natural process. It can work for you. As you read this book, and both contemplate and practice the teachings given here, you will start to realize that the constantly changing circumstances of life are not insurmountable obstacles to your true happiness and the wisdom of enlightenment. Actually, recognizing the transitory nature of reality is a first step to reconnecting to that forgotten but inherent quality of your true nature—your Pristine Mind.

Fortunately, Pristine Mind is already present in all of us. It is not something we need to acquire. Nor is it something that ever leaves us. It is here now, ready to reveal a serenity, vibrancy, strength, and inner peace that most of us have never known possible.

Most people, of course, do not understand the human mind from the helpful perspective of Pristine Mind, and so they suffer from mental and emotional discontents, such as stress, anxiety, and depression. They identify themselves with the ordinary thinking mind and its activities. Indeed, many people believe that the thoughts and feelings they continually experience are what they themselves actually *are*. They believe that without their thoughts and feelings, they do not even exist. They do not know that these thoughts and feelings obscure and cloud the fundamental nature of the human mind—Pristine Mind.

In today's world we are constantly bombarded with all kinds of experiences and impressions, whether from our immediate surroundings or various media. These experiences intensify the feelings, ideas, thoughts, and reactions that make up the "mental events" of our ordinary mind, blocking our view of Pristine Mind. Through Pristine Mind meditation, we can actually see that these mental events obscure a fundamental mind that is powerful, serene, and fearless.

Pristine Mind practice frees us from the constraints of our mental events and reveals transcendent truths about the nature of the mind so profound that our very perception of life is completely transformed. This is a reality experienced directly, not a mystical feeling or a theoretical concept. This wondrous change will not seem obvious until you experience it for yourself. The implications of this deeper subjective experience may strike you as nothing short of miraculous.

The few paragraphs I have just shared with you have no doubt raised many questions. Pristine Mind is not something you can just hear mentioned and then automatically experience. It requires both an understanding and a practice that must be applied with sincerity and effort. But if you receive the right instructions from a qualified teacher, beneficial results can be experienced in a relatively short time.

One thing that people often ask is how Pristine Mind practice differs from "mindfulness" practice. Mindfulness training is a method of working with the mind that has gained a significant following around the world in recent years, producing wonderful results in many settings including schools, businesses, and prisons. The practice has a calming effect on the mind that produces great benefits. It reduces stress and enables people to function more effectively. Mindfulness develops concentration and single-pointed focus, which is very important and, in and of itself, an excellent thing.

The Pristine Mind teachings also include mindfulness techniques, but these techniques are only *part* of the practice. Pristine Mind practice goes way beyond mere relaxation of the mind. It facilitates very important and unexpected insights into the nature of the mind itself, thus enabling a profoundly liberating experience. Pristine Mind meditation accesses an expansive state of mind, one with an immensely broad perspective. We are able to see the mind itself and the whole world as they truly are. We witness firsthand how our ordinary mind creates its own distorted sense of reality. It helps us see how all these experiences, or "mental events," block our awareness of a pristine experience that provides a very different sense of our connection to the world around us. We discover a clear, rich, and beautiful perspective on the world.

This wider, deeper view affects all aspects of our lives. Before long, our new perspective enables us to see how petty our ordinary mind is, how needlessly fearful it makes us, and how prone it is to getting lost in the swirl of everyday events.

When we begin to understand this and see the unimpeded view of the truer, clearer, and more vibrant reality of Pristine Mind, we are filled with gratitude, love, and compassion, which make us feel truly connected to our world and all living things. The fleetingness of life—our enjoyments, our possessions, and even our close relationships—are all the more cherished for their impermanence. Negative thoughts and feelings lose their power to control our lives, and instead give way to appreciation for the gift of our humanity and compassion for the suffering of others.

Perhaps most important of all, we develop a new relationship with our own mind. Once uncovered, our Pristine Mind becomes our refuge at all times and in all circumstances.

Everything we experience is totally different when we engage in the world from the vantage point of Pristine Mind. It is a straightforward and direct connection to the world, without filters, walls, or barriers. Our Pristine Mind meditation leads us to eat, sleep, and breathe Pristine Mind—to operate from Pristine Mind, engage in the world with Pristine Mind, hold conversations in Pristine Mind, take vacations in Pristine Mind, and enjoy myriad sensory experiences with Pristine Mind.

Operating in daily life from Pristine Mind is a way of living that is a thousand times more effective than operating from ordinary mind. There is no stress when you talk to other people or engage in the world this way. This is not just a theory; it becomes your true experience—really, genuinely true.

What do I mean by really, genuinely true? In Pristine Mind our experience is a steady reflection of who we really are at our core. We are self-sufficient and complete, compassionate, happy, loving, robustly connected to the world around us, and unafraid of the unpredictable nature of life. We are not required to renounce or turn away from the world. On the contrary, in Pristine Mind we are genuinely in touch with the world, and we are able to function far more effectively in it.

In the pages that follow, I will teach you the lessons of Pristine Mind and show you the profound practice that can help you gain access to this most extraordinary state. As you read, I would like you to keep in mind an important principle: Do not simply *read* the material—also take the time to *contemplate* it. In doing so, you will be able to use the teachings to explore your mind more deeply than you might otherwise be able to do. I strongly encourage you to read this book slowly out loud, ideally with another person or a group. Reflect on what is said and compare it with your own experience. Soon you will notice a difference in the way you feel, and you will start to move closer to the wonderful experience of Pristine Mind. This will create new feelings of love, gratitude, and fulfillment within you. It is this life-transforming experience that I wish for you.

I will explain what the enlightened masters of my lineage have understood about the true nature of our mind, the qualities of this pristine state, and the reasons we have lost our connection to Pristine Mind.

The very idea that there is such a state of mind may seem quite foreign to you at this point and may raise many doubts. That is understandable. Most people have not experienced such a state. The Pristine Mind teachings are not a dogma, ideology, or belief system. The teachings require no blind faith or suspension of rational thinking. They are simply a practice of working with the mind. I ask you only to keep an open mind; if questions come up, hold them while you continue your journey through this book. The answers will come.

It is also important to know that a mere intellectual understanding of Pristine Mind will not be sufficient for you to access your Pristine Mind. Access to your Pristine Mind and the benefits of Pristine Mind can only be achieved through the practice described in the parts that follow. However, a mental comprehension is necessary and important so that we can understand both the practice and why we are doing it. Without this comprehension to guide us, the practice may feel arbitrary, perhaps meaningless. It is much more difficult to do it correctly if we do not understand *why* we are doing it.

Thus, please be patient and think carefully about what follows. First, I will give you a sense of what Pristine Mind is like and how it differs from our ordinary mind. What we call the "ordinary mind" is what most of us now experience as "our mind" with which we closely identify. Right now, for most of us, it is simply what life is. The basic point I will make is that we are out of touch with Pristine Mind because our ordinary mind functions in a way that obscures and blocks our awareness of it. I will show you exactly how that happens. Access to our Pristine Mind, however, enables us to find true security, serenity, majesty, and meaning in life.

To be completely, truly happy, we must reconnect with Pristine Mind. That is what these teachings are designed to do.

So, let's begin!

PART ONE

Pristine Mind: Our Fundamental Nature

The luminous nature of mind, like the changeless sky,
Is unaffected by temporary events.
—Bodhisattva Maitreya

1. The Beauty of Pristine Mind

AT ITS CORE, our mind is pristine. Pristine Mind is a beautiful, naturally vibrant state, brimming with life, self-sustaining in its capacity to provide a dependable, inexhaustible source of happiness and joy.

Sadly, most of us do not realize the true nature of our mind. We have become disconnected from it. Pristine Mind becomes obscured by the mind's misperceptions and inner experiences—thoughts, feelings, beliefs, and judgments—that pollute its true nature. As a result, we live in a mind that leaves us insecure, alternating between times of happiness and sadness. This robs us of the ultimate experience of life, deeply connected and aware of this pristine state of mind.

In Pristine Mind we are not detached or withdrawn from the world. We do not need to reject worldly pleasures. In Pristine Mind we are far more present to the world than we have ever been before. We experience life's pleasures more robustly, work more effectively, and, above all, love more richly and more universally. Living in this way does not leave us dry and disconnected, but fills us with gratitude and energy. Our very life changes from one of fending off fear and despair to one of contentment, love, and splendor.

Fortunately, this happy state is in us right now. It is who we really are, so we can never really lose it. But in order to rediscover it, we must look for it in the right place. Any quest for unconditional happiness must begin with our own mind.

The Poor Man and the Treasure

My teachers and their teachers before them have contemplated and experienced Pristine Mind through meditation, and over many generations until the present day they have imparted their realizations to countless people. Their most fundamental understanding is that lasting happiness cannot be found by changing our external circumstances. Outer changes may feel good for a short time, but they do not last. Lasting happiness comes only from exploring our inner world and discovering the treasure that is our Pristine Mind. When we experience this treasure, it does not change with the constant shifts of external life. It is always there and accessible to us, no matter what is happening outwardly. After all, it actually *is* us, our true being.

Among the many teachings I have received since I was a little boy, one that I always remember and frequently contemplate is Bodhisattva Maitreya's parable of the poor man and the treasure. A very poor old man lived in a dilapidated hut with very little food or money. He had barely enough to survive. His only possession was a lumpy, uncomfortable bed. As he lay each night on that bed, he stayed awake in great pain at the thought of all that he lacked. "I'm so poor. I have nothing." He was depleted with fear and worry.

As the old man struggled every day to beg for enough food or coins to survive, he fantasized that he could one day be rich. At the end of each day he returned to his hut, often empty-handed, exhausted from begging for food or work. He sat despondently on his lumpy bed and wallowed in the agony of his poverty. He spent his entire life this way.

Sadly, the old man did not know that, while the outside world did not provide him with what he wanted, right in his own home, hidden under his rickety old bed, was a trunk containing a huge treasure of gold coin, enough to provide for him through any hardship. The old man was so busy thinking of himself as destitute and looking for wealth in the world outside that he never explored the very space he occupied most of the time. If only he had looked carefully under his own bed, he could have realized that he had always been rich. Then he could have enjoyed the treasure that had in truth always been his from the beginning.

We are all just like the poor man in this story. In so many ways we seek our happiness from external sources. No one seems to direct us to look within, and even if they do, we get little guidance about what that means or how to go about it. Fortunately, there are differences between us and the poor old man in the story—life-changing differences, if only we take advantage of them.

First, right now, for whatever time we have remaining in this life, we have a chance to look at what is right under our nose and experience the vast riches that are potentially ours if only we can connect to the treasure that is inside us—Pristine Mind. Life is limited, so we do not have forever to do this. But we do have this moment right now and whatever time is left, if we do not waste it.

Second, our treasure is even closer to us than the trunk hidden under the old man's bed was to him. It is actually hidden right inside us at this very moment. It is already there. There is nothing to build or create. It is a supply that will never be empty.

Our human life does not have to be wasted like the old man's, if we look inside, using the understanding and techniques that the teachings provide. To do this properly and successfully, however, we must give the matter more than the passing interest of an armchair reading of this book. We must act with determination, and practice the techniques leading to the rediscovery of our Pristine Mind.

To find the treasure, we must look within, not without. These teachings show us how to look within and find our Pristine Mind.

As you will see, to follow these teachings does not require you to adopt beliefs that contradict your our own independent judgment about reality. You only have to develop the motivation to gain a better understanding of your mind through direct experience. You must first relax the mind and then observe it with patience and perseverance. It is that simple.

THE TRUE NATURE OF OUR MIND

Pristine Mind is the mind we were all born with, our natural mind. It is called Pristine Mind because it is untouched and unspoiled by experiences. It is inherently and permanently pure. It is like pristine land that has not been altered by civilization.

In Pristine Mind our senses are vibrant and alive, our perceptions pure. Things that cause us fear or insecurity in our ordinary mind do not affect us negatively when we are in Pristine Mind, because of its innate serenity. As we gain confidence that it is always with us, our fearlessness increases.

Pristine Mind is not dependent on the ups and downs of life that we have no control over. It just "is." Changing life events that we take so seriously in our ordinary mind are far less significant in the changeless Pristine

Mind. Clouds in the sky may appear, move, change, or dissolve, but the sky never changes. In the same way, the events in our ordinary mind may change, but our clear, spacious Pristine Mind never changes. That is one of the most fundamental things we come to realize about our Pristine Mind.

Bodhisattva Maitreya says:

> The luminous nature of mind,
> like the changeless sky,
> is unaffected by temporary events.

This beautiful verse is very reassuring, especially once we have the experience to affirm it. When we look beneath the surface thoughts and emotions of our ordinary mind, and connect with our Pristine Mind, then we have an inner experience that is constant. It consists of vitality, beauty, peace, majesty, and joy.

Pristine Mind is a state that has been experienced and described for centuries by many who have practiced these teachings. It is not something they have created or made up, nor is it anything we need to fabricate. It is a natural, normal state that is present in all of us. It is something we are born with.

As our true nature, Pristine Mind is our birthright. It has, however, been obscured, covered over, one might even say "polluted," to such an extent that our access to it is blocked, leaving us with our much more limited ordinary mind. Tragically, most of us go through life thinking our ordinary mind is all there is. This is "normal," we think.

This ordinary mind that we are all so familiar with is to us like our breath, something we take for granted. It is just "what our mind is" or "who we are." And we assume that the experiences we have within the confines of that mind are just the nature of life. Most of us have never even considered the possibility that Pristine Mind exists, let alone been aware that it could make such a dramatic difference to our happiness.

Given how accustomed we are to the experiences of our ordinary mind, despite what I have just described, the very idea of Pristine Mind may sound like a fantasy, something distant and hard to attain. It is not. Pristine Mind is not mystical, esoteric, or beyond the understanding of most people. It is not just for monks, yogis, and mystics. It is something we can all access, under the right circumstances. It is an experience that is already inside us, but it has been obscured by our mind's distortions, such as anger, fear, resentment, and other mental events that now block our access to it.

The mind-set in which most of us now live, our ordinary mind, is not "normal." In fact, it is terribly abnormal. If we want to take the true measure of our mental health, we should compare it with our Pristine Mind. In the same way that physicians measure our physical health with their modern instruments of diagnosis, we can measure the health of our current mind by comparing it with how we feel in Pristine Mind. When we experience the changeless and wonderful nature of Pristine Mind, we will see that the feelings of anxiety, boredom, or despair we typically experience are actually deviations from true life. It is Pristine Mind that is the healthy, "normal" state of mind.

Before medical science developed our knowledge about the nature, detection, and treatment of disease, people showed symptoms that often could not be traced to an accurate cause. Without understanding the cause, we typically could not create an effective treatment. In the same way, without these teachings, people may know they are unfulfilled, but they do not know the cause of their unhappiness or the appropriate treatment. Without a known cause and without an effective treatment, one cannot recover from the abnormality of ordinary mind.

At the heart of the teachings is our discovery that inside all of us there is a Pristine Mind unscathed by life experiences, awaiting our rediscovery. Unlike our ever-changing ordinary mind with which we are familiar, Pristine Mind is not a changing or fluctuating state of mind. It is stable and at the same time, boundless. In Pristine Mind we enter into a fundamental state of mind that is brilliant, clear, and tranquil. It is not needlessly affected by either our past or our future. It does not change with the changes in our circumstances. It is extremely attuned to the present and generates great richness of experience from being so attuned.

Until we see what Pristine Mind meditators have seen—both the nature of Pristine Mind and how to access it—we will be left with this ordinary mind with which to contend with our ordinary lives. Unfortunately, that will be a fruitless quest, since the ordinary mind uses self-defeating patterns that simply cannot provide us with the complete happiness we seek. Despite our efforts, it more often only leads us further away from happiness.

When we rely exclusively on our ordinary mind, our search for happiness takes place in the chaotic and arbitrary-seeming world that most of us now experience. It is a world we perceive to be driven by a series of events we get caught up in, within which we live and seek happiness, but which, in truth, is a rat race to nowhere. The Buddha called this *samsara*, a Sanskrit word that means an endless cycle of pain and pleasure, happiness and sadness, that results from a misperception of reality. It just circles around and around, never getting anywhere. It is filled with hopes and fears, and produces very little lasting or deep happiness.

Most people think that samsara is reality and that's all there is to life. With Pristine Mind meditation, you will learn that life offers much, much more than you ever imagined.

2. The Eclipse of Pristine Mind

Iᴀᴀ ᴏᴜʀ ᴍɪɴᴅ is innately pristine, why don't we experience that in every moment? There are three reasons for this. First, we are unaware of our Pristine Mind—we don't know of its existence. Second, we are lost in our mental events, which therefore obscure the presence of Pristine Mind. And third, we identify with our mental events as our normal state of mind. Thus we are unable to reconnect to Pristine Mind by ourselves, without the proper instructions on how to do that.

At this point you probably have several more questions. Why are we disconnected from Pristine Mind? Why can't we find happiness by using our ordinary mind? Why does it seem so hard to reconnect to Pristine Mind, if it is really already inside us? How did we lose contact with our Pristine Mind in the first place?

To answer these questions, we must understand three related forces that obstruct our experience of Pristine Mind: mental events, primordial fear, and the ego. Together they disrupt our connection with Pristine Mind and dominate our lives. They block our way back to Pristine Mind.

Mental Events

We have said that it is our mental events—the thoughts, emotions, feelings, and other experiences that occur in the mind—that disconnect us from our Pristine Mind. Mental events create a complex web of perception and experience that obscures our connection to our Pristine Mind and makes it difficult to reestablish our connection to it. We enter into a dynamic pattern that takes us further and further away from our Pristine Mind and causes much of our fear, anxiety, and discontent. It is this pattern that the Pristine Mind teachings enable us to reverse.

This requires some explanation.

As most of us will quickly recognize, ordinarily our mind processes a tremendous number of thoughts, ideas, emotions, feelings, beliefs, and other experiences—all the things that are our "mental events." If you will take a minute to watch your mind, you will see that there is a constant parade of mental experiences and perceptions that march, dart, lumber, or float across your mind like clouds passing across the sky.

Many of these mental events grab our attention. While we fixate on all these mental experiences, in fact they are often just recollections of a past that is dead and gone, or speculations about a future that may not turn out the way we imagined. Even if they seem like impressions about what is happening right now, on examination we see that they are conceptualizations based on the past or the future. As they swarm over us, they obscure the enduring, stable, and empowering Pristine Mind, which would otherwise give us a beautiful experience of the present moment, unpolluted by conceptual thinking. This is like the way storm clouds obscure a sunny blue sky above them.

When we are born into the world, our minds are uncluttered by many mental events. There are few mental events because the mind of an infant has simply not had many experiences yet. We are born with relatively few habits, views, feelings, emotions, or experiences. We do not yet have many thoughts at all. Our experiences are very limited.

As we grow and develop, however, our mind is soon bombarded by experiences that come both from without (all that we see, hear, touch, taste, and smell) and from within (our thoughts, feelings, concepts, and ideas). The specific content of many of these mental events depends in part on our family, the friends we make, the schools we attend, and the belief system in which we are raised. Regardless of the specific forms they take, however, the mental events all distract us and disconnect us from our Pristine Mind.

They create mental energy waves. The more our attention follows after those waves of mental energy, the more the mental events are reinforced and gain momentum. As they gain momentum and magnetize our attention, we drift further away from Pristine Mind.

Early in this process we are like a small child who is playing at a picnic with her family, enjoying the sun, games, and ice cream. While she is perfectly content at the park, she spots some butterflies a few feet away from the blanket and starts to follow them. She chases them here and there. They are not moving very quickly, and their wings are ever so delightful, so she follows them along a few more steps. Eventually she looks up and finds herself in completely unfamiliar territory, with tall trees and dense forest, and has no idea how she got there.

Just like the child, we get lost in mental events. We get increasingly fascinated by our mental events. Soon, it is no longer just small waves of mental energy that we are following. Now we are completely entangled in an increasingly complex web of thoughts, emotions, beliefs, feelings, and experiences, all those mental events that are now far beyond our control. The more we fixate on and pay attention to these complex mental events, the more intricate the web of complexity that we generate. We become trapped in chewing over our past, pondering our future, and always thinking, thinking, thinking, creating concepts and developing mental patterns about what's going on.

We become unaware, distracted, and separated from the experience of Pristine Mind. Instead of experiencing our Pristine Mind, we are consumed with mental events. This is how the distortion of our mind develops. The accumulation of various mental events becomes so extensive that it completely hides our original Pristine Mind. They cover over our permanently joyous, untainted state of being, which now becomes engulfed by the sea of emotional and cognitive events that we think of as who we are.

All aspects of life are subject to these attention-grabbing eruptions in our mind that are constantly arising and falling away. These experiences, these mental events, constantly clamor for our attention. The rapid pace of change in our world, and the increasing demands made on the mind to be more and more preoccupied with external stimulations and the mental events to which they give rise, only further isolate us from the experience of Pristine Mind.

Once we are disconnected from Pristine Mind, the resulting void in our consciousness is quickly flooded by the vast and ever-changing sea of mental events, and this becomes for us the entire universe of our ordinary experience, our familiar life as we know it. These events are disparate: sometimes fleeting, sometimes capricious, sometimes habitual, sometimes obsessive. Certainly there is no way to corral these runaway horses of the mind, or force the flood of mental activity into a mold of happiness that would be anything like the joy of Pristine Mind that is already present in its perfection. All this confusion may leave us feeling beaten down by life. But our thrashing about in frustration and our efforts at controlling our life with our ordinary mind become increasingly futile.

With all that has been said about our disconnection from Pristine Mind, it may sound as if Pristine Mind is a distant, unreachable experience on some other planet. But Pristine Mind is not an alien or otherworldly reality. Both ordinary mind and Pristine Mind are our own mind; the difference is that Pristine Mind is our mind in its pure, pristine state. It's like the difference between a cup when it's clean and when it's dirty. It's the same cup, in two different conditions. One is the perfect vessel in its original condition; the other has its original purity obscured by stains. Drinking tea from a dirty cup is the same as living in the world with our ordinary mind, which has become distorted and polluted. Drinking tea from a clean cup is the same as living in the world with our unpolluted Pristine Mind.

PRIMORDIAL FEAR

I vividly remember an incident from my young boyhood. My father took me to visit someone at a gathering away from our hometown. There were lots of people around. I somehow got separated from my father. Suddenly I realized he was not there. I began crying. I still remember very clearly the unfamiliar place and the unfamiliar faces all around me. I was torn from my secure world and felt lost.

Whenever we become unwillingly separated from the familiar, we become fearful. Without the awareness of our Pristine Mind, we experience an even more fundamental insecurity than that of a child gone astray.

When we are unknowingly disconnected from Pristine Mind, we are not even aware that we have lost our stability of mind, in which we can remain unaffected by life's unavoidable conditions. The very nature of existence is marked by constant flux. Nothing lasts, everything eventually dies or decays, and fluctuating mental events that continually rise and pass away make life unpredictable. But in Pristine Mind, this fact of life does not upset or imbalance us. In losing access to this stability of our Pristine Mind, we lose our capacity for true happiness and well-being.

When we are in touch with our natural pristine state of mind, then we are comfortable, relaxed, connected, and complete. We are intimate with the universe. But when we fall out of touch with it, we are stuck in our ordinary mind and in a constant battle with an underlying fear, which we can call "primordial fear."

The fear that results when we are disconnected from Pristine Mind is the cause of much of our mental and emotional suffering. It is called "primordial" fear because it has been with us since we originally lost our connection with Pristine Mind. We do not know that there is another experience of the world—Pristine Mind—in which an undercurrent of such fear does not even exist.

In our ordinary mind, mental events arise. The more mental events we have, the stronger our underlying anxiety becomes; the greater the gap between our ordinary mind and our Pristine Mind, the more powerful the anxiety. When we rediscover our Pristine Mind, we realize that this anxiety, our primordial fear, is not inherent to life but actually originates from our disconnection from Pristine Mind and manifests itself in our mental events.

Complicating our predicament even more is the fact that our disconnection from this fundamental aspect of our being can make us feel very exposed and self-conscious. Self-consciousness can be so unpleasant that it creates still more mental events as we search for some escape from it. This in turn only feeds our primordial fear.

Primordial fear manifests in many ways. If you have anxious feelings without an apparent cause, or if you feel uneasy and restless unless you are constantly engaging with other people in person or online, then you are experiencing primordial fear. This fear is why we all try so hard to connect with external things. If we find something that feels pleasant, whether it is a musical sound, an exciting image, something we enjoy touching or tasting, or an object we can purchase and possess, we chase after it because it feels good and gives us temporary comfort at that moment.

The degree of primordial fear that is felt may vary greatly from one person to another. Some, because of their personal history and native temperament, may be only vaguely aware of the underlying fear that feeds unhappiness. Others, who have different past experiences and temperaments, may go through life carrying a great deal of mental and emotional suffering.

Most people are subject to some level of anxiety most of the time, whether they recognize it or not. Many of our activities are in truth efforts to distract ourselves from this underlying primordial fear that drives our ordinary mind and only creates more fear. We make phone calls, create incessant plans, and keep our schedule at a hectic pace. We need the TV on or music playing in the background—even when we're not watching it or really listening—to feel a sense of connection. Even on our way to our activities, we play music as we drive because silence in our car would leave us alone to experience anxiety or boredom.

It is this constant activity around which we organize our lives to avoid confronting our primordial fear. We pursue connection, connection, connection. We try to connect to sounds and flavors and sights. We try to connect to our parents, children, romantic interests, books, or art. We are constantly eating, talking, watching, or listening, trying to connect our five senses to anything we can in every waking moment.

We end up connecting with unreliable objects of attention, whether they are other people, possessions, or diversions. These are unreliable sources of even ordinary happiness because we can't force them to make us happy; and they are ultimately unreliable because of their inherent impermanence. Such is the power and impact of primordial fear.

Distracting ourselves from our primordial fear does not reduce it. Engaging constantly does not reduce primordial fear. Amusements may be a temporary band-aid but not a permanent remedy. Just because we feel hungry does not mean it is always good to eat whatever and whenever we want. If we are eating excessively or choosing the wrong foods, it will ruin our health. In the same way, just because we may currently dislike being still, silent, and by ourselves does not mean that constant distraction is healthy; it takes its toll as well.

There is another problem, however, that we must understand. By running from our fear, not only are we failing to alleviate our separation from Pristine Mind—we are actually amplifying it without realizing it. Distractions generate more and more mental events at an ever-increasing pace. These mental events remove us still further from Pristine Mind. It is another layer of barrier between our ordinary mind and our Pristine Mind. It only makes our road home much more difficult and arduous.

When we lose touch with Pristine Mind, we are ungrounded and unconnected to ourselves and our world. Favorable circumstances will often bring us some kind of temporary happiness, occasional joyousness, and other forms of contentment. But it is not a permanent solution to the problems of impermanence and our general dissatisfaction. Without Pristine Mind, we cannot know unconditional happiness. We become like the poor man who goes out every day, looking for his treasure in the surrounding area, never realizing that the wealth is right where he is. Pristine Mind and the potential for unconditional happiness it provides have been forgotten.

Social anxiety. A particularly distressing manifestation of primordial fear is what we might call social anxiety—not the phobia treated by psychologists, but the underlying anxiety most all of us have about interacting with other people. We think the way we interact with others is normal, but if there is any underlying hesitation, doubt, or discomfort, that is social anxiety. The degree of social anxiety varies among people. A few people are really comfortable; a few are extremely fearful. Most of us are somewhere in the middle.

Turning outward for a sense of security is not just a matter of seeking diversions from various impersonal sources. It also means we look to other people with both hopes and fears. When we are in ordinary mind, our contacts with other people take on an importance beyond what they can realistically deliver. Whether or not we are conscious of it, we hope they will alleviate some of our loneliness, despair, and primordial fear; and at the same time we hesitate to approach others because of fear that our efforts to connect will fail and they will reject us. Attending social events or even just talking with people may trigger our ordinary mind's worry about being judged, our nervousness, our self-doubt, and other negative thoughts and feelings.

In social interactions, most of us seek validation of our own beliefs and judgments. We worry about what other people's thoughts and opinions might be. What do they really think of us? Are we respected, admired, considered "cool" and "sexy"? If people think of us positively along these lines, we feel good about ourselves for a while. But many people are more afraid of others' opinions and judgments than they are of anything else.

Social anxiety comes from being focused on "how we are doing" in this world. We are constantly judging our own performance and others' treatment of us. For example, if we are preoccupied with what other people feel about us, we raise questions: "What are other people thinking? I hope they like me. What are they saying about me behind my back? What do they *really* think of me?" It's these concerns that we project onto others that compound our social anxiety.

If we examine ourselves honestly, we will see that we are constantly making many, many judgments moment by moment. We judge both ourselves and other people. This process influences the way we treat others and, as a result, the way they treat us. Other people perceive the discomfort in us, so they feel even more uncomfortable than they already were from their own social anxiety. Cues go back and forth based on this mutual anxiety and, depending on the degree of anxiety, it can become awkward and stressful. Then we can become even more uncomfortable and more judgmental toward ourselves and others.

If all your attention is on these agitated thoughts, then even if everybody around you appreciates you and says how much they like you, you may not believe it. But when you are in a pristine state of mind, as we will explain in the parts that follow, you have fewer thoughts, and thus less anxiety and fear, because all those uncomfortable experiences come from your thoughts; and without thoughts they can't survive. Then it doesn't matter what people think of you; even if everybody around you hates you, it doesn't affect you. You are comfortable with yourself. Even if everyone glares at you angrily and criticizes you, if you pay no attention to your own thoughts, you remain comfortable and as stable as a mountain. You are completely at ease with yourself.

When we reconnect with our Pristine Mind, we stop the destructive process of projecting blame for our own feelings, either on ourselves or others, so that our family, friendships, work relationships, and social contacts become more stable. At the same time, we are flexible and adaptable. Our primordial fear has calmed down, so rather than having to make judgments about ourselves or other people, or worry about whether we are being treated fairly, we experience the joy of giving to others and relating to them without expectation or apprehension.

Addictive activities. For some people, the powerful cravings of our ordinary mind, and its underlying anxiety, discontent, and lack of fulfillment, can turn into addictive behaviors. It might lead to an alcohol, drug, or gambling addiction in which we compulsively search for temporary and very self-defeating respite from the ongoing agitation. For others, it can manifest in behavior that is considered socially acceptable or even desirable, like the eighty-hour work week of the workaholic. It can also manifest itself less dramatically, like constantly checking e-mail or social media. This behavior turns into a habit, since these distractions can never put the underlying anxiety to rest permanently. These are all forms of addiction—an unfulfilled longing for connection. Like the elusive carrot always out of reach of the donkey, we chase and chase the object of our desire in ordinary mind, but we never really reach it; the very nature of the fear-based and misdirected ordinary mind cannot provide it.

The need for external distractions is like having a food addiction. A person with an eating addiction cannot stop bingeing; they finish the chocolate and then reach for the ice cream, then go out for a hamburger, and then get Chinese takeout on the way home. Mentally, we binge on the stimulation of internal and external activity. It is like we are stuffing our mind constantly. Because our mind cannot stay still for one moment, we do not really see our dependency on the stimulation.

Why do people feel such a strong need for all this stimulation? That addiction to external conditions, that restless energy, is caused by our primordial fear.

It is hard to tell a compulsive eater to stop eating or to eat less, because they are used to eating continuously. Similarly, it is hard to tell ourselves, "Be silent, let go of your thoughts, meditate," because we are addicted to distractions. Our body may eat three meals a day, but our mind eats continuously. As a result, our own internal pristine state continues to be more and more obscured.

Being an addict does not make us content; it makes us crave more. The more we crave, the more we suffer. If we can break the cycle, we will find inner freedom. When we cut through our addiction, we can rest. Enlightenment comes when the mind rests in its natural state. Real contentment is found when our mental events slow down.

THE EGO

As we lose our experience of Pristine Mind, our ordinary, fearful mind begins to predominate. Thoughts begin first, followed by concepts, emotions, judgments, and beliefs. Gradually we identify with each of them as if the experience they create is really who we are. That is when we develop a sense of self. When that sense of self becomes unhealthy, as we shall see, it is called "ego."

In identifying with our mental events, we are constantly looking to our future, analyzing our past, or trying to make sense of what is happening now. We pour tremendous energy into our ordinary mind's processing of mental events. Soon we become firmly convinced that these mental events jamming our mind actually are us. We identify with them and take their appearances and disappearances as reflections of our true identity. What we have taken as "us" or as "our normal state," then, is really a conglomerate of mental events that are, in truth, only superficial experiences, fleeting like clouds.

But we identify with this conglomeration and come to believe it is our essence. If this collection of mental events seems good, we think, "I'm good." If this collection seems bad, we think, "I'm bad." Based on these false identifications, we grasp onto this complex of physical, emotional, and mental experiences in the search for security and fulfillment, hoping it can lead us to happiness.

This is why, at present, most of us believe that our ordinary mind, especially the thinking faculty, perfectly reflects our being. We have no doubt that we are identical with the thoughts and experiences that flutter through our mind, all the mental events that occupy our attention. We also believe that this flow of mental events accurately mirrors the true nature of the outside world, and that our strategies and reactions are perfectly rational, based on these perceptions.

Our sense of self appears when we think, "This is *me*." We build a sense of "what I am." We also develop a secondary sense of self based on possessions: "This house is *mine*." "These are *my* children." "You hurt *my* feelings." If we identify so firmly with this sense of self and our possessions that it becomes a fixation, then we are stuck in ego. This sense of self is very different from the sense of self that we experience in Pristine Mind because it is based on mental events that feel so compelling when we are under the control of our ordinary mind.

Of course, there is nothing inherently bad or undesirable about having a sense of self; in fact, we need a sense of self in order to navigate our way through our day-to-day existence. We need a coherent center of consciousness from which to observe our surroundings, manage our time, and take care of business. However, there is a difference between a healthy sense of self and an unhealthy sense of self. When we are grounded in Pristine Mind, having realized that our sense of self is not who we really are, we can then use our sense of self properly, by thinking, speaking, and acting for the benefit of ourselves and others. When our sense of identity is healthy, even if it involves the use of wealth, fame, or power, it's not problematic but brings happiness and fulfillment for everyone. But when our ordinary mind becomes dominated by a rigid identification with our mental events, or by a need to impose our own thoughts, feelings, and opinions on others, then our sense of self turns into an *unhealthy* sense of self, or ego.

Ego forms when we are so enmeshed in our mental events that we become unduly attached to them. The ego makes a desperate effort to develop a sense of security by building a fortress around our identity to shield it against the uncertainties and changes of life. This fortress is an inherently unworkable structure, because in order to feel secure under this effort, we must maintain constant focus on our separateness from everything around us.

It is difficult to overstate the problems the ego poses for us in terms of both the barrier it creates to reconnecting with our Pristine Mind and the dysfunctional way it encourages us to lead our lives.

The energy we use to create the sense of cohesion that lets us believe that our sense of self is a real entity and not just the assemblage of mental events that it really is, is powerful. In Pristine Mind we free up that energy and use it to experience anew, with fresh eyes, the present world in which we live. In some instances, this can occur suddenly, leading to a dramatic change in consciousness.

More often the change is gradual and our improvement is incremental. It is this transition that requires our time and effort through the meditation exercises that are so important to these teachings. For our purposes now, however, we need to understand that our sense of self is a formidable force holding together our ordinary mind and the experience of the world it creates.

We will discuss a few of the more dramatic illustrations of how the ego operates, but we must remember that the very nature of the sense of self is illusory because it is ultimately not our true identity. We can never be really certain about who we are so long as we pay attention to transient mental events as if they were the reality of life.

Inflated ego. Often we drift off course depending on the nature of our circumstances. When circumstances are good and support us, we are at risk of developing an exaggerated sense of self, a "big ego." Often we do not even notice it. We don't realize that this view of ourselves depends on external circumstances until outer conditions change or deteriorate and different mental events take over our consciousness.

There is nothing wrong with pursuing fame, power, or wealth with the right perspective and good intentions, and nothing inherently bad about enjoying good circumstances. But these conditions and circumstances are ultimately unreliable and unstable. If we become closely attached to these things as integral to our identity, then we can develop an inflated ego. If we identify too closely with a good education, good looks, wealth, or popularity, we are hurt when people do not praise us or reflect back to us their appreciation of whatever we are using at the time to prop up our inherently precarious sense of self. That is why even famous people are sometimes so susceptible to flattery and seem to need such frequent praise and validation.

With any kind of exaggerated sense of self, it is difficult to have meaningful friendships based on an appreciation of our shared humanity. The basis of compassion and love is our fundamental equality with others. We are all in the same boat of life. But when our ego dictates that we must feel superior to others, this equality becomes impossible.

When our ego dominates our sense of self, our behavior, mannerisms, and tone of voice all become expressions of our ego. We may believe that the way we are acting, speaking, and thinking is well received, but people may actually perceive us very negatively, especially when our ego needs clash with their own. They see us as arrogant, selfish, overconfident, and sometimes even dictatorial. We become difficult to connect with, even though we may not recognize it because we so want to cling to this feeling that we are special. We see everything through the lens of "my" and "me." It is hard for others to live with someone who has this kind of ego. There is no true connection with them. It is difficult for everyone around them. This is all a result of the exaggerated ego.

In the midst of living with an exaggerated ego, if our circumstances become challenging and do not support our inflated ego, it feels as if our world is collapsing. It intensifies the threat to our sense of self when our demands are not being met, and this causes us great pain. We have defined our self purely by special circumstances. When these circumstances change and deteriorate, and we feel the world no longer views us in a positive way, we feel lost. It hurts so much because we have lost what we think defines us.

Deflated ego. The exaggerated ego is just one of the two main faces of ego. The other extreme on the spectrum is an unhealthy, deflated sense of self, which is often called low self-esteem. As we noted, our ego is dependent on circumstances and conditions. Therefore, when the circumstances are poor—for example, if we lose our job, fail in something important to us, or are treated miserably—then our sense of self is in danger of deflating. We may dwell on misfortunes in our personal history, such as painful memories of the past or challenging family dynamics. We may focus on how badly we were raised or other factors that evoked feelings of self-doubt, fear, disappointment, or insecurity. A deflated sense of self, due to obsessing over our bad circumstances or shortcomings, is just as egocentric as an exaggerated sense of self. In both cases, we are fixated on our self—either our misperceived superiority or our misperceived inferiority.

Perhaps we have a poor body image or a trait that makes us feel self-conscious. Or we are concerned about our career because we were fired or did not get the job we wanted. Maybe we were rejected by the person we wanted to love us. We may lose confidence, lack willpower, and feel unworthy. We may fixate on that problem and constantly keep it in mind. We may even isolate ourselves and disconnect from the outside world. The more our circumstances are negative, and the more we identify with those circumstances, the worse our isolation and our suffering become.

As long as we have this type of ego, it is hard to accomplish anything positive. We feel impotent and frail. We may become overdependent on others but distrust their motives if they try to help. When an opportunity arises, we do not feel capable of making it work, and this prevents us from accomplishing anything meaningful. And our negative self-perception affects those around us as well, infecting them with our energy of resentment, fear, and cynicism.

In fact, the more we fixate on any sense of self—whether at the inflated or deflated end of the spectrum—as if it were our true reality, the more we reinforce our disconnection from Pristine Mind. In stark contrast, when we are reconnected with Pristine Mind, our sense of self stays healthy because we don't believe the misperceptions and distortions of ordinary mind. Instead, we use our sense of self to accomplish positive things for ourselves and our world.

Effects of the ego-driven mind. Even though ego is an unhealthy sense of self, we often think we need our ego to survive. Some people may even gain success through ego, but the healthiest way to succeed is through a good heart, awareness, and wisdom—characteristics that arise from Pristine Mind. These characteristics should be the driving force motivating our endeavors, not the concerns of our shaky ego. When we are in Pristine Mind, we have the best interests of ourselves and others at heart, and our actions are aligned with reality. Our actions are based on compassion and spring from intelligence and wisdom.

Whenever we pursue a major goal, it is inevitable that some obstacles or problems will arise. How we address these problems will depend on whether we approach them with a healthy or an unhealthy sense of self. A healthy sense of self does not react by serving the needs of the ego; instead, it acts by finding solutions to the problem. But if it is ego that is driving our pursuit of achievement, then as problems come up, our ego only adds to the problems. We end up sabotaging the very purpose of our efforts and alienating others. We hurt other people's egos and then they hurt our ego back. When egos compete in this way, there is no successful outcome for anyone. Ego is a poison to true success, not its driving force.

Ordinary mind perceives the world in a distorted way because the "me" and "my" create an obsession with a false and unhealthy sense of self. That's the reason we have so many reactions of hurt and so much resistance to our circumstances and conditions. In extreme cases, the forces of mental and emotional distorted perception are so strong that they lead to self-destructive behavior. For instance, a number of people commit suicide every year by jumping off the Golden Gate Bridge. They live in one of the most beautiful cities in the world; how sad it is that they are unable to appreciate its beauty or contribute to that beauty. What can explain this despair but the uncontrolled force of extremely distorted perception? Although we ourselves do not go so terribly far astray as in these sad examples, we are influenced every day by our ego.

The more negative thoughts, feelings, judgments, and belief systems we incorporate into our sense of self, the more narrow-minded we become, and the more distorted our perceptions are. When we see the world in a distorted way, we become more reactive. In this state, our Pristine Mind is completely overcast, covered in layers of obscurations. A healthy sense of self means that we have reconnected with Pristine Mind, so we realize that our sense of self is not who we really are. That is the true form of self-esteem and self-worth. When we are in Pristine Mind, our sense of self becomes relaxed and self-assured. We then may maintain a healthy sense of self for purposes of taking responsibility for ordinary necessities such as preserving good health and supporting ourselves and our family, as well as for pursuing enlightenment. We can truly enjoy the good things the world offers, without futilely relying on our ego for happiness.

3. From Discontent to Fulfillment

WHEN WE THINK of happiness, we are generally imagining the good circumstances in our life. We describe how happy we are by pointing to all the good things about our family, friends, relationships, or career. We also claim to gain happiness from hobbies, reading, eating at restaurants, drinking alcohol, watching movies, and socializing; but essentially these activities do not bring contentment so much as stave off boredom. We feel uneasy when left to ourselves with no distractions.

Why do we often get bored when there's nothing to do? Why are we so uncomfortable without distractions? The root cause of our boredom is our underlying discontent and insatiable ordinary mind. We are uncomfortable because our ordinary mind is driven by a hunger, a constant yearning for something. That hunger is lurking around within us, unsatisfied. Without external stimuli, there is nothing to distract the mind from the restlessness of its insatiable thoughts. Our mind is looking for something, but without objects for it to latch on to, it becomes agitated and unsettled. When our thoughts and emotions have a focus, the mind is soothed for the time being. We find a temporary small comfort zone.

This is why we are so in need of distractions. If there is nothing to distract us from the ever-increasing internal agitation, our ordinary mind gets even more restless and generates more mental events that only make the matter worse. We are caught in samsara, in which we pursue the illusion that things external to our mind can give us the security that we have lost because of our disconnection from Pristine Mind.

I am not saying that ordinary enjoyments of life such as amusements, cultural activities, sports, relationships, and social contacts are bad or to be avoided. We may need these distractions until we find ultimate happiness. When a child cries, it may need a toy. But distraction is not the solution. It is a "quick fix," not the permanent solution of unconditional happiness.

You may have a good romantic life. Perhaps you have fallen in love and you act like a teenager intoxicated by endless affection. You feel so good that you might even think that this person is "the one." Suddenly your life seems more meaningful and you feel more content. You are happy for the time being because you have found a good distraction. You are like a child enjoying a new toy. But when that toy is lost, breaks, or gets old, the child goes right back to crying. When the romance of the new fades, the underlying discontent remains.

Even long-term relationships generally depend entirely on circumstances. When times are good, the couple are full of affection for each other, and the partners call each other "sweetie" or "honey." They may tell friends how happy they are and talk about all the things they enjoy doing together or what a perfect child they have. Both partners are unaware of any underlying discontent or emotional unrest while they are in love. The good circumstances are almost like a drug that temporarily makes them oblivious to their underlying discontent.

But what if the tides turn? Perhaps one of them pays too much attention to work and not enough to family, or arguments break out over how much money is being spent. What if their child gets into trouble at school and they disagree about how to handle it? Now they may each feel that their initial happiness has worn off, pointing to these various conflicts as the cause. But the real problem—the underlying discontent of our ordinary mind—has never been recognized and addressed. At the wedding they said how happy they were, but they never stopped to consider that their feelings could change with the changes in circumstances. They may end up in divorce and go on to look for new partners, never having seen the truth—that all relationships are circumstantial, dependent on conditions.

I am not suggesting that relationships, family, vacations, entertainments, and other activities, whether important or trivial, should be given up. In fact, they can be the source of years of great pleasure and satisfaction. But they can never bring indestructible happiness and true contentment. Why should we look for happiness only from circumstances that constantly change when we can uncover a much deeper happiness from within ourselves?

When we lost touch with the pristine state of mind, we developed many thoughts, emotions, and ideas. That loss is the original source of our dissatisfaction. The more thoughts, concepts, ideas, and beliefs accumulate, the more our discontent infuses our life. For example, your thoughts say, "Oh, I need that. Without that, I'm not happy. I deserve something more. This is not enough. Why don't people treat me better? I should get something special." The more your thoughts keep repeating themselves that way, the greater your underlying discontent, because you hunger for some kind of connection—any kind of connection. Whether the connection is through positive or negative emotions doesn't matter as much as the need to be connected to something, anything. But these connections are ultimately unreliable, because they are based on the cravings and fears of the ordinary mind.

To truly solve the problem of our underlying discontent, we need the realization and experience of Pristine Mind. The first step is to perceive that your mind is naturally pristine, and that your mental events are just passing through. You must deeply realize this.

If we remain in Pristine Mind, then we are completely at ease—comfortable, spacious, and very relaxed. Our thoughts and emotions are quiet and peaceful. When our thoughts and emotions are quiet, when the mind is pristine, nothing is lacking, so the hunger that drives mental events has ceased to lurk. Without that hunger, we are comfortable.

We do not need external chatter, preoccupations, or amusements to be happy. Without distractions, we are connected, cheerful, and calm. And even if we are engaged in the world, external experiences are no longer distractions, but genuine enjoyments, forms of happiness, because they are not motivated by internal fears or cravings. When we go to a buffet for dinner, if we are famished, we will devour everything we can grab to satiate our hunger. If, however, we are already well fed, then we can enjoy our food and sample new tastes. In ordinary mind, we are starved for external satisfactions. In Pristine Mind, we enjoy the gourmet cuisine of life.

THE SEARCH FOR COMFORT ZONES

With every blink of the eye, with every breath, we are trying to find comfort—some kind of relief from the underlying agitation and unsettledness of our ordinary mind. We look to family or friends, to some source of stimulation, or to an infinite number of other external conditions that we hope will help us. When we listen to music, watch movies, or engage in any other form of entertainment, in one way we are enjoying it, but in another way it is also an example of using our ordinary mind to find comfort. Our search for this comfort arises from the primordial fear within our ordinary mind.

We are all trying to find a comfort zone, and when our circumstances inevitably change and we are no longer in a comfort zone, our secure and hopeful world is gone. Even when we are getting what we want, we worry that we may lose our comfort zones. We worry about losing our job, our family, our relationship, our health, and anything else that temporarily provides that zone of comfort. We worry that these things will collapse. We think, "What will I do if he breaks up with me?" "How will I deal with losing my job?" "What will happen to me?" And, indeed, some of these things do come to pass. If we depend on these circumstantial events for our security and self-confidence, we are truly vulnerable.

We go through our whole life like this. At first we are young children with so many toys to fascinate and distract us. Then we grow older and go to parties. We feel, "Oh, yeah, I'm funny. People like me. I'm happy." Then we fall in love and spend all our time with our partner. Then we think we want to get married and have children, so we get married and have children. Then we are satisfied with our life, feeling that we have accomplished something. These are the comfort zones we find throughout our lifetime.

With all of these steps in our life, we may be building some contentment, but it is circumstantial. In the end, we don't gain anything. We gradually lose everything we own, our family and friends around us go their own ways or pass away, and even our own body grows old and frail. Our temporary comfort zones don't provide deep solutions to our dissatisfaction.

Once we are in touch with Pristine Mind, however, we discover an internal true comfort zone. Then, even if our outer comfort zones collapse, we are still content and do not experience the fear and pain of loss that we do in ordinary mind.

When you truly experience your mind as pristine and flawless, when you know your pure awareness, your true consciousness, when you recognize and remain within that, then deep down you are mentally, emotionally, and spiritually fulfilled. You are intimately connected with who you really are and with the world.

As your meditation progresses, then your own thoughts, emotions, and mental chatter slowly dissolve, giving you contentment and satisfaction. Then all relationships you have with others are enhanced, and when those relationships come to an end, for whatever reason, you remain fulfilled because you are not entirely dependent on circumstances. You are not merely numbing yourself temporarily to feel content; your contentment is springing forth naturally.

Then any relationships you have, any trips you take, any parties you attend, any sensory experiences you enjoy, are enhanced by your innate happiness. Then whatever you do is more grounded. Then those things are no longer distractions; you are experiencing true happiness. When your mind is pristine, external conditions actually arise as manifestations of happiness, not distractions.

In the parts that follow, I will describe how to find a comfort zone within, how to find ultimate, changeless happiness, how to achieve ultimate fulfillment with your mind remaining present in its pristine state. In particular, part two is about how to realize our Pristine Mind. Part three is about how to maintain our Pristine Mind. Once you achieve or experience the pristine state of mind, then while distractions and entertainments may appear very beautiful, even without those distractions you are still happy and content.

4. TURNING THE MIND TOWARD ENLIGHTENMENT

WE HAVE COVERED a lot of material in this first part. First, our fundamental nature is Pristine Mind; that may seem to be merely a concept right now, but meditation will make it clear. Second, our mental and emotional situation, our ordinary mind, appears to be who we are due to the contamination of our mind by the mental events that result from disconnection from our Pristine Mind; that may also seem conceptual right now, but again, meditation will clear that up as well. We need to begin the meditation process. But before we do so, we need the inspiration, enthusiasm, and determination to make it work.

The enlightened masters of my lineage have provided the pure nectar of the teachings in an unbroken stream, from Guru Rinpoche Padmasambhava all the way down to my own sublime teacher, Jigme Phuntsok Rinpoche. Among these great teachings are four fundamental facts of existence for us to contemplate, to give us the inspiration, enthusiasm, and determination that we need. These facts are as true now as they have always been.

First: the rare and precious opportunity of human birth. Of all the living things in this world, how many of us are human, with a consciousness endowed with the capacity for self-reflection, the ability to ask ourselves what life is all about? Reflecting on this fact enables us to take productive actions, to appreciate every moment we have, to think about how we can help ourselves and others. We should take advantage of this opportunity during this exceptional human lifetime. We possess the power to impact our own lives as well as the lives of those around us—either positively or negatively. It is up to us whether we choose a positive or a negative path, but we should recognize that the choices we make will greatly influence our level of happiness and fulfillment.

Second: the changeable nature of existence. We and everything that exists are impermanent and subject to change at any time. We all know that we will die; we just don't know when. Everything in our world is subject to creation, growth, dissipation, and disappearance. Even our sun and all the stars of the universe will burn out eventually. Nothing remains the same. Therefore, the changeable and uncertain nature of everything must be accepted and dealt with. The Pristine Mind teachings provide a truly effective way of understanding and working with impermanence. It is crucial to always remember the bigger picture. A mind that is focused less on petty daily happenings and more on what is really important, what makes life truly meaningful, will be successful in reaching a state of lasting freedom and fulfillment.

Third: the consequences of our actions. Our attitudes and actions are subject to the natural law of karma. The Sanskrit word *karma* refers to action and reaction, cause and effect. If our mental attitudes are positive, then our speech becomes positive, and our facial expressions and our energy naturally become positive, projecting positive energy, creating positive circumstances. If our mental attitudes are negative, however, then our speech, our behavior, and our body language become negative, projecting negative energy, creating negative circumstances. That is cause and effect, or karma.

Each positive or negative action or attitude has a corresponding consequence or result. It creates a wave. If we have a negative, harmful, hateful attitude toward ourselves, others, or the world, we leave little room for feelings of happiness, and we send waves of counterproductive energy into the world that creates disharmony. If, however, we have a positive attitude with positive intentions and motivations, they too send waves. Through our body language, speech, and facial expressions, and through our very presence, we send the world a very different signal. We make room for happiness within, and we send a more harmonious, beautiful energy out into the world, and that creates many positive, harmonious results. That's the natural law of cause and effect. It is up to us to decide whether the nature of our actions will have consequences that are positive or negative. This fact places a great deal of responsibility on each individual. If we choose thoughts, words, and actions wisely, we will reap the benefits of the goodness we send out into our environment.

Fourth: the discomforts of existence. The nature of our life is a mix of pain and pleasure. Sometimes we feel lucky and other times we feel unfortunate. Sometimes we feel bright, shiny, and proud, and other times we feel dull, withdrawn, and ashamed. We often do not live with the robustness and joy that we would like and that we somehow sense *should* be part of something so precious and miraculous as a human life. Being born, we cannot help passing away, and during our life we have to deal with sickness and old age—if not our own, then of those around us. We struggle to overcome or avoid these conditions, and as a result we suffer mental and emotional turbulence. We often don't get what we want, and we sometimes get what we don't want. The Buddha said that when pain ceases, we feel pleasure, and when pleasure ceases, we feel pain. This is the nature of ordinary life.

When we fully understand these four fundamental facts and incorporate them into our way of living, we do not become egocentric about any impressive achievements we have attained. We understand that such achievements are enjoyable and fine for the time being, but that they are only temporary and short-lived. And when circumstances go downhill— even if we sink to the depths of misfortune—we are not depressed, because we know that the bad times are temporary as well. That's just the way life is. Things change. This realization keeps us from despairing when hardships come our way. Understanding these basic facts, we are better able to handle the hard times. When we realize these facts and make them central to our approach to life, then we become broad-minded and less centered on our ego.

If we base our life on the assimilation and remembrance of these facts, then our view, our outlook on life, is grounded in reality. Otherwise, if we are constantly pitting our self-centered feelings against others' feelings and against actual reality, we will continually run into conflict. And so much human suffering comes from this kind of conflict. It is a clash of the inevitably conflicting ego needs of different individuals, which are ever-changing even for the people involved. If we see the big picture, we have a view that is much more in line with reality.

Best of all, the contemplation of these fundamental facts ignites our desire for enlightenment. This desire itself yields multiple positive experiences and positive mental events. Without this basis in reality, even our positive emotions have no lasting power, because they can't be sustained, and negative experiences inevitably follow. But with these fundamental facts forming a basis, we have the motivation to practice Pristine Mind meditation and to attain complete enlightenment.

5. FINDING HAPPINESS WITHIN

I F OUR MIND is polluted, dominated by negative thinking, then circumstances, no matter how good they are, cannot make us happy. They
do not have the power to uplift us. If we become focused on the negative,
then no circumstance has the power to bring happiness. If water is contaminated, even if we put it in a nice glass and add a lemon slice, until we
purify that water there is no way we can make it delicious or healthy. Just
as we need to purify the water before drinking it, the first thing we need
to do for a happy, healthy life is to purify our mind.

As we have seen, most of us try to find happiness by changing our circumstances. We may travel to a distant land, fall in love with someone new,
or get a better job, but in truth, there is usually nothing wrong with our
lives as they are. Most of us have everything we need—except the inner
knowledge that yields absolute happiness. If you look in a mirror and see
that your face is dirty, you can't expect a different mirror to show it looking clean. What you see in the world is a reflection of your mind. You
can't change yourself by changing the world. You need to change your
mind; then the world reflects the change of your mind. The great teacher
Mipham Rinpoche said, "The foolish person chases after happiness. The
wise person creates the right conditions for happiness."

The reason for our unhappiness is that we have negative perceptions,
negative thoughts. It is because of the undisciplined way we think and
perceive. Of course, the world is not perfect. There are many problems.
But if we pour the negative parts of the world into our minds every day,
then we will be miserable. The less we have that negative mind-set, the
freer we are, the more we enjoy life, and the more we can make positive
contributions to the world.

As our state of mind gets clearer, as our negative thoughts, perceptions, and habits diminish, our happiness increases. If we want to experience happiness, we must work to put our mind in the best place by allowing all the toxic information in our mind to fade away. It is most important that our mind be relaxed and calm, fresh and open. Then we appreciate and enjoy everything, and we feel gratitude. Then also the energy of our relationships flows smoothly.

Pristine Mind meditation enables the natural dissipation of our mind's pollutants. All beings are pursuing happiness in every direction. Instead of looking in every direction, if we take away the barriers to our Pristine Mind, then we are *unconditionally* happy. All we have to do is take away the toxic states of mind, the mental pollution.

To achieve all this, we first need to attain *realization*—revealing our Pristine Mind. We then need to practice *meditation*—journeying deeper into Pristine Mind. While doing so, we must develop a *good heart*—connecting with the world in the best way. These are the topics that follow. If we do this, we will accomplish ultimate happiness, what we call Enlightenment—the fully awakened Pristine Mind.

PART TWO

Realization: Revealing Our Pristine Mind

The vividly clear present moment of unceasing awareness is
primordially perfect enlightenment.
If we realize this, we instantly become enlightened.
Therefore, please do not become distracted.
Look at yourselves and see who you really are.

—Guru Rinpoche Padmasambhava

6. The First Aspect of Realization
Who We Really Are

So far, we have explained how our mental events, discontent, negative emotions, distorted perceptions and ego result from our losing touch with our Pristine Mind. We talked about how our ordinary mind developed from our primordial fear. Now we can discuss the solution to all these problems—uncovering, or realizing, our Pristine Mind. By rediscovering our Pristine Mind, we can know who we really are, without mental distortions, with a healthy sense of self. So now we can begin the treatment for the discontent, the negative thoughts, and the misperceptions of our ordinary mind.

Calming the Mind

On a cloudy day, when all we can see are clouds, we cannot see the blue sky because the clouds obscure our view. Yet the luminous, beautiful, and boundless sky is always there.

As we have described, in the same way, if our mind is busy, chaotic, confused, or agitated, we cannot see our natural state of mind. Under these circumstances, we don't realize that behind these thoughts and other mental events, our mind is calm, beautiful, boundless, and fearless. We do not realize that this is who we really are.

Mental events are like the clouds in the sky. If our mind is constantly churning with mental events—thoughts and emotions, beliefs, and habits—it is impossible to experience the mind's natural pristine state. For that, our mind must be calm and our view of the mind must be uncluttered by transitory, but insistent mental events.

Even if we appreciate the importance of calming the mind, however, we will not be able to do that unless we know how to meditate properly.

When our mind is cloudy, we cannot access Pristine Mind. But when our mind is clear, with the help of meditation we have the opportunity to realize who we really are. With that realization our life changes in a way that we never imagined possible.

You may be skeptical about this claim at first. Many people have a hard time even believing in the possibility of such a thing as Pristine Mind. Instead, they think that all there is, is the mind they know already, their ordinary mind. The reason for this is simple: they have never meditated, or they have not meditated properly, so they don't have any other way of understanding their mind. But when they start Pristine Mind meditation, their ordinary thoughts subside and Pristine Mind appears—and then confidence in the reality of Pristine Mind is born.

So our first step is to learn the proper way to meditate. We have to know the appropriate technique, and we need to apply it properly to calm our thoughts and experience our mind in its pristine condition. Our attention is always directed to the external world. Now is the time to look within. Only then can we begin to realize the true nature of our mind.

Guru Rinpoche Padmasambhava says:

> If you want to go sightseeing, try touring your own clear,
> mirrorlike mind instead.

The Runway to Pristine Mind

What technique can we use to effectively start our journey to realizing our natural, pristine state?

The clearest instructions for doing this come from Guru Rinpoche Padmasambhava, the main architect of the Pristine Mind teachings. Guru Rinpoche has given us the essential opening instructions for practicing Pristine Mind meditation in four steps:

> Don't follow the past.
> Don't anticipate the future.
> Remain in the present moment.
> Leave your mind alone.

We must understand these instructions. They are designed to help us stay in the present moment. Some other forms of meditation teachings say that remaining in the present moment is the ultimate objective of meditation. However, the present moment itself is not ultimate reality, ultimate truth, or the ultimate goal of Pristine Mind meditation. Nor is it what I mean when I refer to our fundamental nature. Instead, being in the present moment, with our mind calm and relaxed, simply creates the right conditions to begin to connect with our Pristine Mind.

We can think of abiding in the present moment as the "runway" to Pristine Mind. To fly an airplane into the sky, we need to take off from a runway. The present moment is the runway from which we take off to enter into our natural state of mind. But it is important to understand that remaining in the present moment just by itself is no more like being in Pristine Mind than sitting on the runway is like flying.

When I first began to travel by plane, it was very unfamiliar. I had never been on an airplane before. The plane needed to accelerate to a certain speed on the runway before it could take off. Then it would begin to rise into the sky. This was a new experience for me. I felt a little bit anxious and uncomfortable, especially during those first few minutes after takeoff when there is often a little turbulence. It felt very unnatural and strange to me. No one could move around or use their electronic devices. Everyone needed to keep their seat belt on.

After a while, however, when the plane arrived at its cruising altitude, people took off their seat belts and moved about. The flight attendants began to serve refreshments, and we discovered that we could then relax and enjoy the flight.

It is like this when we meditate. For someone who has never meditated before, who has never rested their mind, it can be a similarly unnatural experience. We may initially feel anxious or claustrophobic. We have a restless energy that makes it hard to remain in the present moment.

When we first start to meditate, the mind is pulled back by the heavy weight and number of thoughts and emotions that fill our mind and preoccupy us. There is significant agitation while the mind continues to be caught up in these mental events.

Initially, we go through all sorts of turbulence that makes it hard to remain present. We cannot rest our mind, because we have to go through that turbulence for a few minutes, just like on an airplane. As with the plane taking off, however, if we try to remain present, there is turbulence only for the first five to ten minutes. In time, our internal experience changes. Our initial agitation subsides, we relax, and we abide in our increasingly comfortable and more natural state. We gradually remain more and more in the present as the mind calms down. Eventually, we arrive at our internal cruising altitude, and we, too, can "relax and enjoy the flight."

This is the difficulty many people feel when they first meditate. They often feel quite discouraged. However, this kind of initial experience is absolutely normal and does not mean that we are failing at meditation. Nor does it mean we are not benefiting from what we are doing. If we keep practicing, soon we will find that the turbulence passes, just as it does on the airplane, until we reach our more comfortable cruising altitude.

GUIDED MEDITATION: THE REALIZATION OF PRISTINE MIND

Let's go through a guided exercise showing how to actually start meditating.

Preparation. To prepare to follow the four steps given by Guru Rinpoche Padmasambhava, begin by relaxing your body, speech, and mind.

To relax your body, sit somewhere comfortable, such as on a chair or a cushion on the floor. Make sure your body is comfortable and at ease, not tense or awkward. You don't have to try to maintain an unfamiliar, stiff position.

Next, relax your speech by allowing yourself to be quiet. Just relax into silence. Breathe naturally. Don't force, control, or regulate your breathing.

Next, relax your mind. This is the most important part of this preparation. Your mind must be relaxed and present. This does not mean it should be passive and dull. Instead, it should be aware and alert. Keep your eyes open. Don't shut out what you see, hear, or think, but don't pay attention to those things either; just be natural in your keen awareness of your mind. In Pristine Mind meditation there's no need to shut anything out. This gets easier as it gets familiar, like learning to ride a bicycle.

Step one. The first step, after this initial preparation, is *don't follow the past.* Do not get caught up in thoughts, memories, or images of your past, regardless of whether they occurred minutes ago or years ago. Bring your mind fully into this present moment. Focusing on and following past events empowers the thoughts and emotions that disturb us. By not focusing on the past, we can quickly dissolve many of these disruptive thoughts. They slowly disappear from our perception.

Our mind has many outer layers of such thoughts, emotions, and other mental events that obscure our Pristine Mind. If we are going to fully realize the truth of our fundamental nature, we must stop following thoughts of the past. If we follow them, we are simply creating more mental events that lead us further away from realization of our Pristine Mind. Paying no attention to our mental events and not creating new ones is the first step in dismantling the layers of mental events that cover our Pristine Mind.

Step two. The second step is *don't anticipate the future.* Remind yourself that now is not the time to pursue, plan, or follow any thoughts, feelings, or imaginings of the future. Do not begin wondering or speculating about what will happen. That is just another way to invite mental events. Instead, just stay alert in the present.

At this moment, then, while you are meditating, your mind is neither in the past nor in the future. It is not held hostage by mental events based on memories of the past or projections of the future. That means the mind is clearer and calmer. You have dismantled more and more of those layers of mental events that block your Pristine Mind, and, as a result, more of your Pristine Mind is slowly exposed to your view and realization.

Step three. When you are not in the past and not in the future, then the next step is *stay in the present moment.* Just be present. There is nothing to do but vibrantly experience your mind. The question is not what to do. Your mind is just being natural and aware. Just let your mind be natural in this way. Just as water is just water, and blue sky is just blue sky, your mind is just what it is, remaining in the present moment.

It is important to note here, however, that being in the present itself is not a passive and lifeless process. It is not simply "spacing out." That will do little good. Instead, it is an active and dynamic process, not unlike the airplane going down the runway and taking off. In the beginning it requires some effort. As you move into your meditative cruising altitude, it is more tranquil, but still vibrant.

Apart from this, you do not need to do anything but be who you are.

Water does not have to try to be water. It does not have to try to be calm, clear, and liquid. Water is innately still, clear, and calm. That is what water is. The blue sky does not have to do anything but just be the blue sky. The sky does not panic when the clouds are gone; it just remains the blue sky. Similarly, when thoughts and emotions subside, you do not need to panic. You do not need to wonder what you should do. You just need to allow your mind to be what it naturally is. Simply experience your awareness. Observe only the clarity of your mind. Nothing else is necessary.

Step four. Finally, Guru Rinpoche Padmasambhava says, *leave your mind alone.*

You don't have to expend effort pushing thoughts of the past or future out of your mind in order to remain in the present. You don't have to drive thoughts out of your mind and grasp at the present moment. Instead, just let all those thoughts melt away, leave your mind alone, and the present moment will be there for you. You will gradually feel a lightening up. Your thoughts will fall away, as if you are rising into air. Your thoughts will settle like sand in a glass of water.

If you meditate properly and are able to leave your mind alone, all ordinary thoughts will subside because your mental events cannot survive without your attention on them. How can they survive? Your current thoughts and emotions originated from your attention to the past and the future. Now that you are no longer paying attention to the past or the future, the thoughts and emotions naturally dissolve.

We know that clouds cannot exist without the presence of certain circumstances. If no such necessary conditions are present, then clouds cannot continue to exist. They just vanish. They are gone. Similarly, if there are no supportive conditions for thoughts or emotions, then they, too, just vanish. When clouds dissolve or disappear, only blue sky is left.

The spacious blue sky of our mind has always been present, but it has not been visible, because there are so many clouds of mental events obscuring it. As mental events dissolve, our Pristine Mind naturally emerges. This is our fundamental nature. This is the ultimate reality. This is the true nature of our mind.

When we experience Pristine Mind, we are more ourselves, our mind is more natural, and that state is less obscured and less disrupted by mental events that cloud our view. When we are in that condition, we see our naked mind without the clothing of mental events.

In facilitating that increasingly clear view of our mind, this meditation leads us to "realization"—a realization of what our mind truly is and who we really are.

Once thoughts and emotions subside, we are left with the experience of Pristine Mind. You need to experience it for yourself. And this meditation is the way to accomplish that.

When you have meditated for a while, you can check for yourself. Is your experience more pristine, calm, and clear? Does it feel boundless? Is it "flawless awareness"? Is it free from distortions? Is it an untainted state?

Experiencing your mind directly in such a way is experiencing your fundamental nature. Everything that you need to understand is explained clearly right there in that experience.

If you understand and know who you are in this state, then you will experience the most amazing and beautiful thing.

> The mind is like a blue sky, fundamentally; eventually you will discover that.
> The mind is flawless; eventually you will experience that.
> The mind is pristine, pure; eventually you will directly enter that.
> This is the most wonderful thing that will ever happen in your life.

You realize or recognize your true state of mind, your normal, natural, unfabricated state of mind. Perceiving or experiencing your true nature is called realization. The more you meditate, the more this experience will unfold. As Guru Rinpoche Padmasambhava says:

> The mind's own awareness is naturally brilliant, like the sun.
> To see for yourself if this is true, look into your own mind.
> Your pristine awareness is continuous, like a river.
> To see for yourself if this is true, look into your own mind.
> The various events of mind cannot be found, like wind in space.
> To see for yourself if this is true, look into your own mind.
> Whatever you perceive is your own projection, like your reflection in a mirror.
> To see for yourself if this is true, look into your own mind.
> Your thoughts naturally occur and naturally dissipate, like clouds in the sky.
> To see for yourself if this is true, look into your own mind.

This is just the beginning, but it is very, very important. The entire path to full awakening, or enlightenment, starts here.

When we stay in Pristine Mind meditation for twenty to thirty minutes, or longer, we are on the path to experiencing that fundamental mind, not the ordinary mind full of mental events. We are coming face to face with the fundamental, natural state of mind that is otherwise obscured by the mental events that usually preoccupy us and consume all of our attention. We must not just understand this intellectually, but we must actually perceive that pristine state and experience this state of flawless awareness for ourselves, face to face.

As we attain this realization, we see our awareness without layers of distortion. We recognize, "My mind is innately flawless. I never saw that before." It's like seeing the sky without clouds and saying, "Oh, I see. The sky is blue." It's not an intellectual concept—it's experiential. We have that kind of experience. We see that our mind is pristine.

This kind of realization in meditation is the key that opens the door to enlightenment. It all starts here.

Guru Rinpoche Padmasambhava says:

> If you recognize your own innate pristine awareness,
> You will surely attain enlightenment.

With our increasing understanding and steady practice of meditation, we will find that when our mind is cloudy or irritable, we can return to our calm, pristine state instead of following our mental events, and then all mental events will dissolve. With more and more experience, whenever we feel agitation, sadness, or stress, we can just return to this pristine state. Whenever we are anxious or afraid, we just return to this state.

When we come back to this state and we remain in pristine awareness, our negative experiences vanish. This pristine state becomes our normal experience. We can dissolve those uncomfortable experiences at any time. As our practice grows, this becomes our new normal experience. At any time, we can access Pristine Mind merely by relaxing ourselves—not following the past, not anticipating the future, staying in the present moment, and leaving our mind alone. Of course, when we are not in formal meditation, we need to deal with our everyday circumstances. But more and more, we will be able to maintain our awareness while doing so.

Reconnecting with our true state of mind is the most important, most precious, most valuable, and most liberating experience in the world. This recognition determines everything that is to come. Not knowing, realizing, or recognizing our true nature leaves us confused and at the mercy of our thoughts and emotions. Being aware of our own fundamental nature leads us to the happiness and liberation of enlightenment. If we want to free ourselves from the experiences of mental events, primordial fear, and ego, we take the most important step toward that freedom by experiencing the realization of Pristine Mind.

Guru Rinpoche Padmasambhava says:

> How ironic that we have not recognized something that has
>   been with us for so long.
> How ironic that even though it's as clear and brilliant as the sun,
>   it is something so few people ever see.
> How amazing that no matter how much happiness or suffering
>   we experience, our Pristine Mind never changes.

Realization is the recognition of our Pristine Mind. When we experience realization of our natural state of mind, that connection to our Pristine Mind is restored. With realization, ordinary thoughts and emotions diminish, our fear gradually dissolves, and our sense of self becomes healthier and more robust. Eventually we recognize that remaining in Pristine Mind is the essential solution to all of our problems in life.

All these improvements come from our realizing our Pristine Mind. From this first realization, the journey to liberation begins and the distortions of our ordinary mind lessen and lessen. What unfolds is the path to enlightenment.

It is important to understand, however, that our ordinary mind and the unhealthy ego that often controls it do not easily give up their power to dictate our thoughts and perceptions. As a result, some people may resist the very idea of realization because of their own beliefs or the belief systems or "conventional wisdom" that they have accepted as true. They may even make improbable claims based on their own thoughts, opinions, and beliefs, and try to convince others that what they believe is true for everyone. Established religious systems, for example, have their own belief systems. They often want their own views to be accepted as true by everyone.

Once you have experienced Pristine Mind, you do not have to blindly accept either your own current set of beliefs or others' opinions and judgments about what is true or not true. Instead, you will see for yourself what is true. When your thoughts and emotions vanish, when you perceive the actual nature of your mind, then no one's opinions, judgments, or views are involved. That direct perception is called *realizing* who you really are. It is realizing your own natural state of mind, the way your mind has always been.

In meditation, we are realizing the nature of our own true consciousness. When our thoughts and our belief systems subside and fall away, then we have access to the person we really are.

A question I am sometimes asked is, "How can we take care of our daily lives if we are focusing only on the present moment, and not on the past or the future?" During meditation, we don't entertain these thoughts. Afterward, of course, we attend to the practical issues of life, which necessarily require planning for future contingencies and considering past events. When we cook, we cook; when we drive, we drive; and when we meditate, we meditate.

A beginning meditator may not experience Pristine Mind immediately. This is because a beginner may be unable to remain in the present moment and to leave the mind alone. These are the most important things to do when meditating: to remain in the present moment and to leave the mind alone. This takes practice. When you find your mind wandering into thoughts about the past or future, just bring your attention back to present awareness. The more you do this, the better you will get at it. Then your Pristine Mind will appear naturally.

7. The Second Aspect of Realization
Who We Are Not

W HEN WE HAVE ordinary, unenlightened perception, we see and perceive thoughts and emotions as just who we are. We think that our ordinary mind—our thoughts and emotions and the swirl of events in our mind—actually make up the "I" we speak of when we refer to ourselves.

Once we have directly perceived our Pristine Mind, that direct perception gives us a chance to experience the second aspect of realization: that thoughts and emotions are just mental events, not who we really are. When we see who we are, we automatically see who we are not.

The more we remain in that pristine state of mind, the more we perceive all mental events—whether happy or sad, angry or desirous, positive or negative—as just passing across our mind. This aspect of realization is a direct, personal, firsthand experience of that reality, not just something we learn intellectually.

Once we have become really familiar with the experience of Pristine Mind realization, no matter what kind of thought or emotion or other mental event arises, we no longer identify with it. We see any agitation in our mind as just a passing event. We think, "I know my mind is innately pristine. These experiences are just events passing through." We perceive them that way. We do not have to say this out loud to ourselves. We just begin to naturally see things that way once we have had some degree of realization of this truth.

THOUGHTS AND EMOTIONS ARE LIKE CLOUDS IN THE SKY

Once we realize the nature of the sky, once we realize and perceive that the sky is always naturally blue, then we automatically realize that clouds, rainbows, pollution, fog, and other things that appear in the sky are all just passing events. We see this automatically once we realize the nature of the sky as it truly is behind the cover of clouds.

In the same way, once we perceive and experience the natural state of mind, the pristine state of mind, we appreciate that all thoughts, emotions, and experiences are just events passing across our consciousness. They are not who we are. Our natural state of mind—who we really are— is our Pristine Mind, which has been obscured by our preoccupation with mental events.

And once we have really seen it for ourselves, we will always be aware of it. Once we realize the sky is blue, we don't forget that realization just because the sky is sometimes cloudy. If it is a rainy day, we automatically know that clouds and torrents of rain are temporary. Later it will clear up because the true nature of the sky is clear, blue, and beautiful. We always have that realization.

Similarly, once we develop some certainty in our recognition of the natural state of mind, whether we are meditating or not, when any events occur in our mind—whether happy or sad, good or bad, positive or negative, whatever thoughts or emotions occur—then we always know, "This is just an event occurring in this moment. It is not me or who I am. It will pass." That's just how we will always perceive things to be. If we have the first aspect of realization to some degree, then the second aspect of realization comes automatically, and it allows us to treat all thoughts and emotions like rainbows, like clouds. We are no longer distressed by them in the way that we once were.

MENTAL EVENTS ARE LIKE INTERNAL DEMONS

If we do not know that our mind is pristine and that all our thoughts and emotions are just mental events, we are unable to deal with them effectively. As long as we believe our mental events are "me," as long as we believe "I think, therefore I am," they hold sway over us. When we believe that mental events are the source and framework of our sense of self, then they are like a dictatorship that we always need to obey and always treat as the established order, just the way things are. We do not have a choice. It's a totalitarian state. In this state our thoughts, emotions, and belief systems dictate our life and control us because we think they make up who we are. This misunderstanding is the cause of suffering for many people; they cannot overcome their suffering, because they believe their mental events are their identity. To them it is an unrecognized given that their thoughts and feelings are their entire being.

Oftentimes we bombard ourselves with negative thoughts like "I'm not good enough. No one understands me. No one loves me." Those thoughts create much of our suffering. Such thoughts are internal "demons" because they create so much mental turmoil.

Until you know how to experience and abide in Pristine Mind, your thoughts and emotions are like monsters or demons taking control over your mind. These thoughts and emotions, especially those involving desire, anger, pride, and jealousy, can be pictured as having multiple hands and mouths, always hungry, always grasping, always wanting to devour or destroy something external, projecting that changing these external circumstances will provide some comfort. Your thoughts and emotions are always searching for some thing, some place, some situation, some person, some circumstance to occupy your mind. They constantly project onto objects, thinking, "Without this, I'm not happy. If I don't get rid of that, I won't be happy." If you believe your thoughts and emotions, and accept their way of finding a comfort zone, then for the rest of your life you will always be looking, searching, yearning. Where does that voracious appetite for gorging or annihilating external circumstances originate? Nowhere but your own thoughts.

The *Essence of Secrets Tantra* says:

> Thoughts are the real demons. Demons come from your
>   own mind.
> When you know that your mind is pristine, then even the name
>   "demon" no longer exists.

Most people's problems spring from their own thoughts. Their thoughts, their mental events, create unhappiness, disturbance, and chaos in their relationships and in other areas of their lives. That's why thoughts are the real demons, because they are the cause of suffering, chaos, separation, and conflict in so many areas of our lives. They may not be the external demons we can picture with horns, fearsome gazes, forked tongues, sharp teeth, and giant claws, but thoughts are much more destructive than the most gruesome demon.

Generally, we identify with our mental events and carry them with us throughout our lives. We just keep accumulating mental events without any respite. We overvalue and even cherish our own thoughts. Some people even take pride in their thoughts. But as long as we cherish and protect our ordinary thoughts, there is no liberation, there is no freedom from our suffering, because the thoughts we take so seriously dictate our experience. In such a thought-created world, it does not matter if we are rich and famous. It does not matter if we can travel into outer space. It does not matter if we live in the White House. We are always the victim of our own thoughts and the experiences they create for us.

As long as we believe our mental events are who we are, we cannot control them. They demonize our life with thoughts such as "He doesn't like me" or "People don't appreciate everything I do for them!" or "Why do bad things always happen to me?" We are filled with judgments, worries, needs, and fears.

However, when you know how to access Pristine Mind and you remain in Pristine Mind, then your thoughts lose their power. They slowly vanish, and your mind becomes comfortable and fearless because your demonic thoughts have disappeared. Your mind is so tranquil, so blissful.

When we know our mind is pristine, there are no internal demons attacking us. We find that our life in Pristine Mind is stable, with no necessity to thrash about in the thought-based confusion of ordinary mind. Therefore, the way to tame and pacify our internal demons is to know that our mind is pristine and see that our thoughts are only mental events.

Once you have rediscovered your Pristine Mind and you have become familiar with it, then even if you are distracted by external sights, sounds, or perceptions, they don't affect the essential beauty of your existence. Your mind is pristine, so you experience the pristine nature of everything. Mipham Rinpoche describes this by saying that external conditions, distractions, and all kinds of mental events become your allies—they are no longer the enemies of your natural mind. Then, when you abide in your Pristine Mind, you remain happy; and when you have the inevitable distractions of life, you are also happy.

Once you know how to rest in Pristine Mind, and can maintain that state by relaxing and remaining within it, then all external experiences arise as extensions of that pristine experience. They have no effect on your fundamental comfort.

The solution to every problem is knowing how to remain in Pristine Mind. Focusing on a statue or image of the Buddha, or praying to God, or finding satisfaction in external distractions may be helpful in some ways and for some time, but finding your pristine awareness is everlasting. The only thing that is truly yours is your own pristine awareness.

A CHANGE IN ATTITUDE GIVES US A CHOICE

Once we realize our pristine state of mind, our attitude toward mental events shifts. Now, when mental events occur, we realize they are just passing events; they are not who we are, nor do they possess any independent reality of their own. That reflects a shift in our perception. We no longer feel compelled to tolerate thoughts and emotions or be controlled by them. We see that they are transitory. We do not define ourselves by them, because our attitude has changed. Then our experience of life no longer has to be shaped by those mental events.

They do not have the power to pull us along in their direction. We can stand on our own and have some independence from them. We have a choice to say, "No, I do not agree to let that be my experience. You have controlled me for too long. Now I know that you are just travelers passing through. I do not need to invite you in." When we discover this truth, that we truly have power over how we experience life, it is a wonderful, liberating experience.

This liberation is caused simply by the shift in our attitude toward mental events. As we have seen, our subjugation to mental events is the source of suffering, unhappiness, problems, and conflict. But with the realization of Pristine Mind, we develop a different attitude toward mental events. Part of that attitude is recognizing that we can change our internal experience of life. This is a great reward for us—far better than winning even a great honor like the Nobel Prize.

When we see, hear, and feel things that evoke negative reactions, it's because our mind is distorted by its lack of realization about mental events. How do we know that our mind is distorted? Fear, anxiety, anger, stress, jealousy, cravings, and egocentrism are some of the many symptoms of mental distortion. The undistorted mind no longer experiences these thoughts and feelings, even when the outer stimuli are the same.

With realization, we do not act as if thoughts and emotions are negative or bad, because we do not see them that way. We simply no longer see them as powerful. It is when we do not know their real nature that they seem negative, powerful, controlling, or demonic. Once we know their true nature, and know that we can be free of them, they are less threatening. We realize and experience that what were once our internal demons are just passing events, nothing more, nothing less, like scattered showers, mist, or even thunderstorms. But if we hold on to these mental events, whether positive or negative, they become bigger and bigger until they completely overcloud our Pristine Mind.

That habit of holding on to mental events is happening every moment of every day—the idea that some bad thing happened, that memory from long ago, that news we just saw on TV. While these experiences are just projections of our own distorted mind, the tighter we cling to them, the more real they feel and the more they dominate our experience of the world. Without the realization that these mental events are really not part of our fundamental nature, we do not recognize our choice. Through meditation we begin to realize that we do have a choice that we never dreamed possible before that moment of realization. When we have realization and can experience the natural state of mind, everything we see becomes like a dream, a show, or a movie. In the same way that we can just watch a movie, we can just watch whatever mental events arise in our mind. We see them, but we do not get stuck in them.

Once we have the first realization, that our mind is pristine, then we can let go of those mental events, knowing that they are separate from our natural, permanent mental state. Do we want to remain immersed in those patterns and events and the experiences they subject us to? Do we want to hold on to them and the suffering they cause us? Or do we want to just observe them and let go of them? There is space between our mental events, on the one hand, and who we are, our natural mind, on the other, just as there is space between clouds and the blue sky above them. We can separate who we are from these mental events and let the events pass away.

When I was young in Tibet, I often watched clouds in the sky. I was in charge of taking my family's yaks out to graze up in the high mountain grasslands near where we lived. The sky in Tibet is so brilliant, clear, and blue that we would stay outside most of the time, especially in the summer.

Sometimes I watched the sky all day. I could see the clouds slowly appear, gather, grow, and slowly disappear. Those clouds appeared because of certain conditions in the atmosphere. But when the conditions changed, the clouds dissolved.

Similarly, when thoughts, emotions, or other mental events appear in our mind, it is because certain conditions have arisen. When we remain in Pristine Mind, the conditions are not hospitable for mental events, and so they are much less prominent in our experience. The more we meditate, the more thoughts and powerful emotions slowly fade away and dissolve like clouds in the sky, revealing the pristine state of mind.

The more we focus on a mental event, the bigger it becomes, just as small clouds can grow until they eventually cover the entire sky in an enormous cloud cover. Then the rain falls.

Pristine Mind gives us a different experience, one that is always there if we attend to it. But we must realize that it exists before we can take advantage of it. That realization comes with sustained practice of Pristine Mind meditation.

CHANGING OUR MENTAL DIET

While many of us have become conscious of the kinds of food we take into our body, we are less conscientious about the kinds of mental events we put into our mind. This is the cause of much suffering and prevents much joy.

One woman who came to speak with me described a number of problems that seemed insurmountable. She'd had an unhappy childhood with parents who treated her poorly, was fearful about everything, and felt that nobody liked her. Several healing rituals were already being performed for her that were supposed to remove the bad energy left by many years of mistreatment. She thought these rituals might help but asked me what else she could do to feel better.

This woman unfortunately had a really poor mental "diet." While external methods can remove the causes of illness and help us heal physically, true mental healing requires us to change from the inside, to shift our perception and thereby transform our experience even of uncomfortable circumstances and events. As long as we perceive and think in ways that make us suffer, as this person was doing, we cannot heal. Changing our mental diet yields the only genuinely helpful results.

If we always eat bad food, it upsets our stomach; until we change our eating habits, it will not clear up our stomach problems. In the same way, if we still have those negative thoughts, beliefs, and perceptions based on past experiences, external healing practices can provide only temporary relief at best. As long as our negative thoughts are still there, they continue to poison our life. Mental healing requires changing internally. The experience of realization that occurs in Pristine Mind is exactly what causes this shift. Without having to forcibly remove negative thoughts from our mind, our realization allows us to let those negative thoughts dissolve like all other mental events. Once we shift internally, healing begins. When our thoughts, attitudes, and our beliefs improve, healing occurs. Those changes are required for us to truly heal.

People generally define themselves based on temporary thoughts that form in their mind. They say, "I'm an angry person. I'm a sad person. I have so many problems. I'm depressed. I'm impatient. That's just who I am." We do not need to define ourselves so negatively. Once we understand the fleeting nature of these kinds of negative mental events, we can stop doing so. Instead, we will know inside ourselves, "These are just mental events. They are all passing. They are all temporary and superficial. They are not powerful. They come and they go; nothing more, nothing less." It is much healthier and more accurate to treat them this way.

Difficult, unpleasant experiences can be simply released, and positive, joyful, productive, good feelings and experiences can be enjoyed. We can choose between the mental events we like and the events we do not like. After we realize that our Pristine Mind is who we really are, and that our mental events are not who we are, we have the power to choose our own mental events.

Once we have Pristine Mind realization, it is like arriving for the first time in a free country, away from the dictatorship of our thoughts. We can choose our own thoughts, emotions, and experiences. If we like them, we can let them stay and increase that positive experience. If we do not like them, we just let the passing mental events dissolve.

CLEARING OUR MENTAL CLUTTER

In our ordinary mind, we live like someone with a hoarding disorder. We have, figuratively speaking, a wonderful house in the hills overlooking a bay with panoramic views of expansive bridges, and in that house a spacious living room with many windows and a comfortable couch from which to enjoy the view; it is a beautiful, comfortable, and wonderful experience. But if we collect all our trash in that house year after year—old newspapers, rotting food, and moldy clothes—it becomes challenging to even walk from the kitchen to the living room because it is so full of junk that we have collected.

This is exactly what we are doing with our mind when we identify with our thoughts and emotions and other mental events; we are hoarders—mental hoarders. We have this beautiful Pristine Mind with five amazing senses that are like beautiful windows to the world. When our mind is pristine, everything we see, hear, touch, taste, and smell is viewed from the pristine perspective.

However, if we store clutter and garbage in our mind, and if we constantly add more clutter and garbage, we are distorting our view of the world. It adds clutter and sluggishness to our mind when we save negative thoughts, bad habits, unhealthy belief systems, and other toxic information in our mind.

As the years pass, we accumulate more bad habits, heaps of negative emotions, and piles of negative thoughts. Then, in whatever direction our mind turns, there will always be something waiting to upset us. That is what it is like in our ordinary mind, which has been collecting self-defeating habits and distorted beliefs year after year.

One of our habitual tendencies is to question every new idea that we are presented with, although we don't bother questioning our old, ingrained thoughts and beliefs. But new ideas and old ideas are all the same from the viewpoint of Pristine Mind. Ten-year-old mental garbage is no more special than new garbage. But in our ordinary mind, we identify with the thoughts and beliefs we have accumulated, and we think, "That's who I am."

Life is very hard when we identify with our mental clutter. But when, through the realization of Pristine Mind, our mental events cease to define us, then we are no longer a mental hoarder. Our mind is not holding on to useless material. Our mind is clean and beautiful.

What is it like if we take out all the clutter that we have been hoarding year after year, clean the house, put in new furniture, and decorate it with beautiful arrangements of flowers and artwork? After we do that, the view is so beautiful that it is a joy to behold. We wonder why we didn't do this a long time ago. And when other people visit us, they feel refreshed and comfortable, and enjoy coming to our home.

If we take the debris away by simply understanding that these thoughts and emotions are passing mental events and not things to amplify by focusing on them, then our own experience becomes very comfortable, blissful, and pristine. Our very own experience becomes consistently comfortable and refreshing. We have created the right mental environment in which to experience the world.

And we have the kind of mind that makes other people happy when they are with us, just like when we have a beautiful house and they say, "Oh, what a beautiful home you have! Thank you for having us here." When we realize our Pristine Mind, other people enjoy us. They appreciate our presence and feel more comfortable around us. Everyone feels happier when our mind is more beautiful. For this to happen, we must clear away the mental debris we have hoarded for so long.

As we cultivate our Pristine Mind through meditation, we are doing just that. The rewards in terms of human happiness for us and for everyone with whom we come in contact are immeasurable. When we learn and experience all of this, we realize how unfortunate it has been that while we have known how to clear out the clutter from our house, we have not known how to do this for our mind. It is infinitely more important to know how to keep our mind clean than our house. With a house, at least we can move out, but with a mind there is nowhere else to go.

Knowing that our mind is pristine, and not clinging to mental events, is the way to clean our mental house. If we are doing that each moment, each day, it means we are keeping our mental house clean, our mind pristine. Once we develop these two realizations—that the nature of our mind is pristine and that mental events are just passing events—then we know how to clean our mental house and restore it to its original state.

When we realize our mind is pristine, our experience completely changes and we feel so much better. We feel mentally and emotionally refreshed, vibrant, and happy. However, as long as we hold toxic mental events in our mind, we tend to feel that many of our life situations are tremendously difficult. These burdensome situations keep returning no matter how often we think we have laid them to rest. Once we know how to let them pass, how to let go of those experiences and remain in Pristine Mind, we become natural again. We can return to our normal state of mind.

One of the most important things you can learn right now is how to recognize a passing mental event, remain in the present moment, and allow the mental event to dissolve. Are you aware that you can actually do that right now? When you begin to experience the separation that exists between the mental event passing through your mind and the actual mind itself, your Pristine Mind, then you begin to see for the first time that you do truly have the option to choose your experience. You learn how to do just that, and it changes your life.

Until that time, however, while people may know how to clean their house, they have difficulty understanding how they can clean their mind. But people can choose to be in an enlightened mind rather than an ordinary mind. That's really what we are talking about here—choosing to live in an enlightened mind that is immeasurably richer than any ordinary mind. We are talking about nothing less than that.

There is a Tibetan saying: "Beings of hell actually cling to their own place." It doesn't matter that it is a place of horrible torment; they are used to it and have grown attached to it. They are reluctant to leave it. Do not become attached to your own inner hell. Know that there is a much better experience available, already inside you, and find it!

ATTENTION: THE POWER SOURCE OF MENTAL EVENTS

Sometimes we might question whether experiencing Pristine Mind and recognizing that thoughts and emotions are just passing events can really help us avoid all the suffering we go through. When we are unhappy, angry, or stressed, we feel as if those moods are real, palpable experiences, not mere thoughts or feelings that we could simply walk away from.

Suppose we do recognize that these mental states are just passing events—is that really enough to help us move out of our mental and emotional turbulence? It's understandable that we might doubt that it could be so easy. We feel as if the negative mental events are in our heart, in our head, throughout our body, in our very chemistry. But the only reason we have those strong physiological reactions and sensations is that we took that thought or emotion very seriously—that is, we validate the experience and give it significance as if it were real. Our attention is absorbed in that experience. In doing so, *we* are the creators of its significance.

When we take thoughts and emotions seriously, we give them power. It can feel as if they are physiological, but they are actually just happening in our mind. The physical sensations, such as a pounding heart, are secondary reactions; they are actually energy waves caused by those strong mental events. When something happens in our mind and we take it seriously and hold on to it, it creates big waves of energy that flow from our mind and cause a physiological effect. Those thoughts and emotions themselves do not have any inherently physical property. We are supplying that experience with our own mind.

Some thoughts and emotions, then, are more powerful than others because we take some more seriously and feed them with more attention than others. The more seriously we take an emotion, the more powerful it becomes. Some emotions are less powerful because we pay less attention to them. The same emotion can be powerful at one time and weak at another because on one occasion we take it more seriously and pay more attention to it, and on another occasion, we don't take the emotion as seriously or pay as much attention to it.

Our attention is the only reason thoughts and emotions are powerful. They do not have any independent power. Our attention and focus on them feed their power. Taking mental events seriously and paying attention to them make mental events powerful. The more seriously we take them, the more we recharge their energy.

Once we realize thoughts and emotions are events passing across our Pristine Mind, once we direct our attention to remaining in Pristine Mind instead of to those thoughts or emotions, once we no longer take those mental events seriously, then they no longer have power. If they do not have power, they no longer have much impact on a mental, emotional, or physical level.

Again, this is not a theory I am propounding to you. You do not have to accept what I am saying on blind faith and then hope for some magical change in how you feel. What I am saying is empirically the way it works. With sufficient meditation practice you will see this for yourself. You will experience it and then know it for yourself.

When we have any kind of strong emotional reaction to an occurrence, we can observe what happens: The more we think about what happened—with thoughts like "Whoa, this is really bad," or "Something is really wrong"—the more we pay attention to these reactions and take them seriously, the worse everything gets. We may even panic.

For example, if we are with a child and we encounter a dangerous situation, and we panic, then the child panics too. We take it seriously, so the child takes it seriously. But if we do not panic in that situation, the child does not panic. He or she is able to remain calm as well.

Our own mind reacts the same way as the child. If we do not take our thoughts and emotions seriously, then we do not have as strong a reaction to them. They do not make us panic or overreact. Knowing that thoughts and emotions do not have any inherent power is tremendously helpful. This allows us to deal skillfully with all mental events—whether they are beliefs, thoughts, or emotions. The next time we experience a troubling thought or emotion, if we do not pay much attention to it, or if we get distracted by something else, we will see that the mental experience disappears.

In general, why do mental experiences disappear? Our attention influences our experience. When we do not pay much attention to them, mental events dissolve. That's their nature: they are sustained by our focus and attention on them. Mental events do not have their own reality. Again, this is an empirical, observable fact, not just a theory.

An important reminder: Throughout this book, when I say that mental events have no inherent reality, I am not condemning thoughts, emotions, or beliefs. I am not saying, "Please do not have any thoughts or emotions. Thoughts and emotions are bad. Do not ever have any thoughts. Do not have any emotions." Instead, I am saying that mental events have *power* if we pay attention to them. I am suggesting that instead of giving power to mental events, we should recognize and abide in our natural state of mind. When we do that, our thoughts and emotions slowly and naturally decrease by themselves, without any deliberate effort, and become more manageable.

When our state of mind becomes more pure, negative thoughts and emotions naturally drift away without any need for us to use any techniques to counteract them, because they just subside naturally. All we need to do is remain in the natural state of Pristine Mind. Then, without our having to prevent them, stop them, or condemn them, they naturally subside. That is their nature. And this is our liberation.

Freedom from the Chains of Beliefs

Beliefs come in many forms. They can be about how we feel about ourselves, our religious and political points of view, our ideas about how to raise children, or our ethics and morality. In politics, for instance, we hold convictions about the role of the government. We may feel these convictions are based on facts, but the "truth" of these facts depends on our point of view. Our thoughts and emotions may change all the time, but we tend to hold on to our beliefs much more tightly.

We tend to be reactive and emotional when something challenges our beliefs, because our mind is held together by those beliefs. We use this rigid structure as a defense against the uncertainties of life. We try to achieve a sense of security through the conviction with which we hold our beliefs.

We hold on to our beliefs tightly, thinking, "This is permanently, definitely, absolutely the truth." We are strongly attached to our beliefs, and we identify with them. That's why it feels threatening when someone has a different belief or when our beliefs are contradicted or challenged.

Beyond our habitual need to identify ourselves through our connection to exterior circumstances, in our ordinary mind we are controlled more by our beliefs than by any other form of mental event. Each culture, each religion, each political party, each individual has different beliefs and opinions about right and wrong, proper and improper. When circumstances do not match our expectations, we can become threatened, angry, and even aggressive. But once we are more relaxed about our beliefs, if we are not invested in our beliefs as if they defined our identity—if we don't consider our beliefs to be who we really are—then the threat recedes and we free ourselves from the chains of beliefs.

Once we see that all activities of mind are just mental events, then we see that belief systems, too, are just mental events. When we establish contact with our Pristine Mind, we do not feel such a need for the illusory security of a belief system. We gain openness, freedom, and insight into the nature of the world. It doesn't mean that we will necessarily change our beliefs, but it will make us more open to examining our own beliefs—even our most basic assumptions about our lives—to see if other points of view have any validity. With access to our Pristine Mind, we still retain beliefs, but we recognize them as mental events, so we are more flexible in our interactions with those who disagree with our beliefs.

8. The Third Aspect of Realization
Mental Events Are Illusions

THE THIRD ASPECT of realization requires careful articulation and contemplation in order to be understood correctly.

Once we realize the pristine nature of our mind and have learned to remain within that pristine state, we eventually begin to understand that our mental events are not the well-defined, discrete experiences we thought they were. Instead, more and more our mental events are discerned to be illusions.

This third aspect of realization means that we begin realizing that any mental events that arise—happy, sad, good, bad, positive, negative, thoughts, or emotions—are projections of our own mind and do not exist independently of it. They are like the illusory magic of a magician.

It is important to see the difference in our experience as we move from the first two aspects of realization to the third. With the second aspect of realization, we still feel as if we need to let the mental events that arise pass by. While we have realized that they are just temporary events, we still attribute a sense of reality to them and feel we still have to endure them or accept them as if they were real. This requires us to exercise some degree of patience to wait for them to pass. That is because we still think mental events are real.

But with the third aspect of Pristine Mind realization, when we realize that mental events are illusory, we do not need to wait for them to pass. The moment anything arises, we realize at that very moment that it is illusory and does not exist as we perceive it. The mental events that once grabbed our attention in ordinary mind lost their tenacious grip on us when we reached the second aspect of realization. With the third aspect of realization, however, they have no impact on us at all. We notice them, but because they are illusory, they do not faze us.

Before we realize this aspect of reality, we are like a small child at a movie theater who believes that what appears on the screen is real rather than images projected onto the screen. Even as adults, sometimes we forget that the movie is not real and we react mentally and emotionally to what we see. As we practice Pristine Mind meditation, however, we know in the deepest parts of our being that any events in our perception are circumstantial, just as a rainbow is circumstantial; not only does the rainbow's existence depend on the circumstances of moisture, sun, and sky, but it also depends on our perceiving mind to make it appear.

The rainbow's appearance is just a perception. It looks as if it is there, but actually it is not really there any more than living movie actors are really on the screen. The movie is an illusion created by the film, the projector, the screen, and our perceiving mind, making it seem real.

In the same way, our mental events do not inherently or independently exist. They come and go easily. They appear and then disappear. Practitioners of Pristine Mind meditation eventually experience that all mental events are illusory; they do not exist independently of our perception. They are insubstantial. They are circumstantial like clouds or rainbows.

Illusoriness is sometimes misunderstood to mean that there is nothing there. If nothing appeared, however, we would not refer to it as an illusion because there would be no object to *be* an illusion. The point of illusoriness is that there seems to be something there, but it doesn't really exist as we think it does. Something appears, and in ordinary mind we are convinced something exists; we are convinced something is real, but what we think it is in actuality does not exist in the way it appears.

It is like a mirage in the desert. Circumstances of heat, light, distance, and the way we perceive things create a vision of a distant oasis with water and green trees, but when we reach it, the oasis is not there because our viewpoint, our perception, has changed. It was an illusion. We experience, feel, see, hear, or touch something, but it is just circumstantial. It doesn't have its own reality. That's why it's called an illusion.

In the very popular Mahayana scripture known as the *Heart Sutra,* the Buddha makes this famous statement: "Form is emptiness; emptiness is form." The meaning of this is that events are illusory events; thoughts are illusory thoughts; emotions are illusory emotions; experiences are illusory experiences; images are illusory images. Realized beings experience everything to be illusory—as not having any existence independent of their perceiving minds. They are not fooled by their thoughts. In this way they move closer to the true nature of ultimate reality. As the Buddha says in the *Dhammapada*:

> Nothing is real. When we see this through our own wisdom, suffering can no longer harm us. This is the perfect path.

As we have seen, in the second aspect of realization, we realize experientially during meditation that if we pay attention to events, they appear to be significant; if we do not pay attention, they diminish, until eventually they vanish. So we see that if we pay attention to our anger and other negative emotions, they grow more powerful; if we do not pay attention to them, they disappear. Now, on further examination, we see that they are all illusory—they don't really exist at all in the way we think they do. The more we abide in Pristine Mind, the more this perception gains momentum. Then we don't need to keep chasing rainbows.

This is the experience of illusoriness. Trying to appreciate this truth through logic or intellectual analysis cannot do justice to its power of liberation. It must be experienced to be appreciated. That experience is available through diligent Pristine Mind meditation.

LOOKING CLOSELY AT THE NATURE OF THOUGHTS AND EMOTIONS

Now we are ready to look at the significance of this third aspect of realization, the illusoriness of our mental experiences.

Let us suppose we see a beautiful rainbow on the far side of a valley, and beyond that rainbow is an imposing mass of clouds. The rainbow is incredibly beautiful as it radiates light and color across the entire valley, looking like a masterpiece of nature's artwork. And we see the billowing clouds that are like mountains looming above us in the sky. The rainbow looks gorgeous and the clouds very majestic when we view them from a distance.

But the closer we get to the rainbow, the more it fades, because there is nothing really there, no solid physical object. Circumstances caused that colorful arc to appear, but if we attempt to approach it, it vanishes, because the rainbow can only be seen from a particular angle. Similarly, the clouds that look so powerful and majestic are not really there either; if we could enter the clouds, we would experience only moisture and mist. What happened to that powerful mass? It was never really there. It only looked that way because of how we saw it. From far away, that distance creates a certain impressive image, but up close, it is just moisture in the air.

In the same way, when we are angry, depressed, or sad, when mental events are overwhelming, we experience those things vividly. For example, if we are very angry at somebody, if we focus on the person we are angry with and say to ourselves, "He is such a jerk. I don't know why he did that. I am so angry," then we get very angry. While we are actually focusing on that person, we feel our anger and resentment intensely. If, however, we shift our attention from focusing on the object eliciting our anger, and instead observe more closely our feeling of anger itself, we see that it is really circumstantial, like the rainbow and the clouds. In that moment, when we simply witness the anger, we may find that our anger ceases to exist, just as the rainbow and the clouds cease to exist as we saw them before, when we move closer to them.

When we do this, the angry energy fades away into nothingness because it was an illusion. Anger is an illusory appearance like the rainbow and the clouds. Circumstances and our perception make that anger appear. When we look closely at that anger, when we focus on the energy of anger and look directly at it, our perception shifts; we see there is nothing really there that we can identify as "anger."

This exercise of looking more closely at our feeling of anger gives us insight into the implications of our discovery that all mental events, including negative experiences like anger and sadness, are illusions. They are just our arbitrary interpretation, a construct that is in our mind because, in truth, everything we experience is circumstantial. This does not mean that our emotion is unjustified and that we must repress it. It means that we look at the emotion from the pure, open, boundless viewpoint of Pristine Mind and know that the emotion is not who we are. The emotion is then manageable.

Our mental events depend on circumstances. They have no inherent existence by themselves but are a function of our interpretation of ever-changing circumstances. Just like the rainbow, which is merely an impression produced by certain circumstances and our viewpoint, the energy in our mind looks like anger from one angle of interpretation, but from another angle, it's not even there. Our idea of reality is a subjective interpretation of ephemeral circumstances that are not what we think they are.

Whenever a mental event makes us feel angry, depressed, or otherwise unhappy, we naively, reactively grab on to the experience as if it were real. When we focus on mental events, we give them energy, and we experience them more vividly as a result. It feels as if they are more compelling and more powerful than they actually are.

We can appreciate this very clearly when we are in Pristine Mind. We have our mental events—our anger, resentment, or desire—but we do not reflexively imbue them with so much significance, because when we more closely observe the feeling itself instead of attending to the object of our feeling, the mental event subsides. In our true being, in our Pristine Mind, we remain calm, content, and fearless. This is not something we are able to do when we identify with mental events and believe that they are an essential part of us. In our confusion, we let them drag our subjective experience all over the place, unwittingly giving them the power to exert control over us. Pristine Mind meditation lets us see and realize all of this in a meaningful way and lets us experience the liberating impact it has on our minds and our experience of our life.

At this point, you may have some intellectual understanding of what we are discussing. It is crucial, however, to meditate in earnest in order to get any significant benefit from this discussion. Otherwise it is devoid of any real meaning for us. With Pristine Mind meditation, when we are angry, sad, or fearful, instead of getting caught up in what makes us angry, sad, or fearful, we look closely at the feeling itself and see that our mental event is illusory. That is what Pristine Mind practice enables us to do. That is what helps us see that our mental events are powerless unless we give them power.

So authentic meditation does not mean just sitting quietly on a cushion for five or ten years, continuing to treat our mental events as real without looking at the workings of our mind carefully. Those who meditate in this way may experience relaxation or some transitory "spiritual" experience, but they are not moving toward the realization of Pristine Mind and eventually to complete, perfect enlightenment.

If we are to benefit from meditation practice, we must do it in such a way that we truly learn who we are beyond our mental events. These mental events are not who we really are. If we think of them as who we are, our life remains insecure and uncertain. In contrast, our Pristine Mind is not caught up in such mental events and helps us live in accord with truth and reality. And there lies happiness. This is why we must understand the nature of illusion.

People with realization know how mental events arise, remain, and disappear. Ordinarily, people do not understand this, so they naively take everything they experience to actually be just the way it seems. They do not know how things appear and are sustained or disappear.

They do not know whether mental events are real or just circumstantial because they do not know how to differentiate the two. They experience what they think is reality and take everything that appears seriously. This makes everything feel real, not illusory. It's like someone who indiscriminately eats anything they are given, without considering the nature of the food. They assume all food is of the same nutritional value. They eat everything put in front of them, but then they look up and say, "I'm sick."

It's similar with people who are still in ordinary mind. Anything that appears to their minds, they get caught up in. A happy moment occurs and they think, "Okay, I'm happy." A sad moment occurs and they think, "Oh, no! I'm sad."

They do not realize that those things are illusions, because the feelings appear so real and significant. So people delude themselves and get entangled in whatever manifests in their perception, believing it is truly as it seems to be. These experiences seem very powerful to people who do not investigate them carefully. But when they do examine them, the closer they get, the more they find that they're illusions—convincing and apparent, but ultimately not real.

Highly realized Pristine Mind meditation practitioners are masters at understanding how mental events appear and behave. They know that when we focus on an outward object, then the mental events appear strong. But if we move our awareness more closely toward the energy of those mental events, they vanish. When we can do this well, we are left with our natural, pristine state of mind.

The more we experience our natural state of mind, the more deeply we know what illusion means—not just intellectually, but experientially. For example, we can try to explain to someone who has never seen an airplane that three hundred people can fly in the sky in a giant gray bird-shaped metal box. We can liken it to a vehicle they are familiar with, like a boat, but for someone who has never seen an airplane, it will be challenging for them to understand. Once they get on a plane, however, they can experience it directly and understand what an airplane is and know that it really flies.

In the same way, when we hear about illusoriness, our habit of assuming that things really are as they appear is so strong that it is hard to convince us that mental events are illusions. This is why illusoriness is very difficult for us to really understand. Even when we gain some intellectual understanding of it, the real meaning of illusoriness is something that has to be experienced through familiarity with meditation. Only after we experience it can our understanding of illusoriness be strong enough to help us remain aware of our Pristine Mind.

The difficulty in understanding illusoriness has nothing to do with what is true or not. Instead, it has to do with what is familiar to us. The unfamiliar is difficult, while the familiar is easy. When we become familiar with the experience that things are illusions, it is no longer difficult. Our ability to understand just depends on which experience is more familiar.

This is why this third aspect of realization is more challenging to accept just from reading about it. Once we gain access to this experience through meditation, it gradually becomes easier to understand and realize in a very profound way. Since things are illusory, not solid and permanent, perceiving their illusory nature is consistent with reality. We are realizing the truth.

To summarize, then, Pristine Mind realization has three aspects: Perceiving the natural state of mind; perceiving that all thoughts and emotions are mental events; and perceiving that all mental events are illusory. These three realizations are the key to unlocking enlightenment, liberation, peace of mind, and both conditional and unconditional happiness. As we develop each of these aspects of realization, our perception becomes more and more beautiful. This is the path to fully realizing our Pristine Mind.

In *The Ornament of the Sutras,* Bodhisattva Maitreya says:

> For those who realize everything is illusory, life is like taking a walk through a park. No matter how successful they are or how badly they fail, they have no fear of negative emotions or suffering.

THE POWER OF ILLUSIONS

If thoughts and emotions like anger, desire, jealousy, and all other mental events are illusions, why do they have such power? It is because we do not realize that they are illusions. We do not know that they are circumstantial. We take them to be real, and in doing so give them power. We do this with anything that appears in our mind, no matter how fleetingly. It has become an ingrained habit.

Mental events do not have any inherent power apart from what we bestow on them with our attention. We perceive them as real, and that perception makes them powerful. Even if something is not real, if we think it is real, then it becomes powerful to us.

Some people believe in the hallucinations they see, the voices they hear, and the paranoia they feel, because those experiences seem so real. But that does not mean that those visions, voices, and feelings are based in reality. They are not. This is an extreme and unusual example, but in the same way, when we have more ordinary experiences such as anger, desire, sadness, or frustration, we take these perceptions seriously because they feel real. We do not realize our mental events are illusory, and in that way they are just like hallucinations. In failing to realize this, we give our perceptions power. Even if it is an illusion, nonexistent, if we think it is real, we make it real.

Certain mental events may predominate in an individual. Some people have a lot of guilt or anger. Some people feel very unworthy, while others have the good fortune to have positive feelings most of the time. Any pattern of mental events that we repeat and become familiar with will become a predominant pattern in our life. Why? Because we feed that pattern and recharge it with our attention. That is why it has power. It is not because that pattern is real. It is just because we think it is real and respond accordingly.

Sometimes people think we are denying or dismissing their emotional experiences if we say that mental events are illusions. They can become defensive. But identifying mental events as illusory is not intended to discount them. Of course, they do seem real, powerful, and able to affect our life. The point is that they are not the way they seem, and they do not have to have the powerful grip over us that we give them. That is why it is so transformative to understand their illusory nature. We can become free of them if we understand that. It is profoundly liberating.

Through understanding and experiencing the three aspects of realization, we align our mind with the truth. Our mind is innately pure and pristine; when we perceive that, we realize the truth. Positive and negative thoughts and emotions are just passing across our consciousness; when we perceive that, we realize the truth. The emotions and thoughts we have are illusory, which means they do not exist in the way they appear and they are completely dependent upon our interpretations. When we perceive that, we also realize the truth. But this is not something to accept on faith just because it says so here. It is something to be experienced through Pristine Mind meditation.

9. The Significance of Realization

Our meditation must be driven by all three aspects of realization: who we are, who we are not, and the illusory nature of mental events. This means we must step outside our lifelong perceptual tendencies. This is how we achieve realization of our Pristine Mind. Once we have realization, we automatically see how limited our own previous tendencies were, and the nature of those limitations. Once we see that our tendencies are limited, not an accurate portrayal of reality, we have made true progress. At that point we are not totally stuck in a world governed by the misperceptions that arise when we give more meaning to illusory events than they really have. As a result, our old tendencies no longer cause us to suffer unnecessarily.

Realization provides guideposts on the path of seeing reality. There is tremendous benefit to this insight. The closer we step toward reality, the more our limited concepts and thoughts gradually disappear, and the lighter, freer, and more buoyant we feel. If we do not begin to have these realizations, we should evaluate our meditation. Even people who spend many years meditating can remain stuck in their own habits. Then their meditation has no power to improve their life. That is why we must follow the prescribed technique and do our meditation diligently and properly. The reward for our doing so is beyond words.

Nirvana Is Here

Samsara and nirvana do not exist somewhere "out there" in the world or beyond. They come from within our own particular mind-set. They originate from our perceptions and perspectives, and are linked to the very same world in which all of us live right now. If we have an accurate mind-set, then nirvana is here, right now, in this moment. If we have an inaccurate mind-set, the wrong perspective, then samsara is here, right now, in this moment.

What is the correct mind-set? It is not just some static or rigid perspective. Having the right mind-set means realizing the natural state of mind, and realizing that thoughts and emotions are just illusory mental events.

An incorrect mind-set is when we think that any mental event, whether positive or negative, is simply who we are. It is also when we believe that our mental events actually exist.

If we believe in this distorted reality, and if we continually think in that way, then we are in samsara, the confused world of delusion in which we endlessly go round and round.

If we have the proper mind-set, then we are in the state of nirvana because we directly perceive our natural state of mind and we know that thoughts and emotions are illusory mental events. We see the truth.

The right mind-set is Pristine Mind. If we have that perspective, then in our experience, nirvana is here. The more deeply aware of that truth we are, the more we increase our experience of it, then the more deeply we experience enlightenment, or nirvana. For someone who has this enlightened mind-set, even if they live in this troubled, confused world, in their experience nirvana is here right now, in this moment.

It is important to note, however, that when we refer to achieving nirvana, it is not really about "achieving" anything that we do not already have. It is about how the right mind-set empowers us to access and experience nirvana easily and directly in the present moment.

Most important, our state of mind determines our reality. We can be living in a beautiful place with beautiful circumstances with everything externally going perfectly, but if we have a distorted mind-set, if we are completely stuck in our deluded experiences or completely caught up in our mental events, then we cannot experience nirvana. Most of the time, we do not even feel ordinary happiness and satisfaction, let alone nirvana.

In contrast, people in Pristine Mind, even those who are in very difficult situations externally, still have peace of mind and tranquillity. Their circumstances do not affect them. They experience them for what they are—illusions without the power to destroy the beauty and joy we experience in Pristine Mind. This is what occurs in nirvana.

SUDDEN AND GRADUAL REALIZATION

There are two different timelines by which meditators can experience the three aspects of realization. In the first, realization occurs suddenly, all at once. When the meditator realizes who they really are, their natural state of mind, they simultaneously realize their thoughts and emotions are not who they are, that they are just illusions.

This is illustrated by a well-known event in the life of Nyoshul Lungtok, who was one of the most devoted students of the Dzogchen master Patrul Rinpoche. Many times Lungtok asked Patrul Rinpoche for Dzogchen teachings, because he wasn't perfectly sure whether he had really realized his pristine awareness. Occasionally Patrul Rinpoche would lie on a wool carpet in the open air, on a hill above the Dzogchen Monastery, and gaze at the night sky, meditating. Lungtok would accompany him, standing nearby, waiting for the next opportunity to receive Dzogchen teachings from his master. On one particular quiet evening, Patrul Rinpoche said to Lungtok, "Sweet Lungtok, have you yet recognized the true nature of your mind?"

Lungtok answered, "Master, I don't really know for sure."

Patrul Rinpoche said, "Come here, Lungtok, lie here next to me and look at the sky." Lungtok followed this instruction. "Do you see the stars shining?" asked Patrul Rinpoche.

"Yes, I do."

"Do you hear the sound of the dogs barking in the Dzogchen Monastery?"

"Yes, I hear them."

"Do you hear the sounds of our own voices?"

"Yes, I hear us."

"That is meditation, dear Lungtok," Patrul Rinpoche said.

With this simple instruction, Nyoshul Lungtok instantly realized the true nature of his mind, and he firmly maintained his pristine awareness ever after.

This is the power of the authentic master: to help the devoted student to realize the mind's true nature. When the master has the necessary high realization about the nature of mind, and the student has the necessary gratitude and devotion—then, rarely, this sudden realization can happen.

In the other timeline, which is much more common, the meditator experiences the three aspects of realization gradually. First, they realize who they are, that their mind is pristine. Then, as they continue to practice meditation, they realize that their thoughts and emotions and experiences are not who they are, but are just mental events that come and go. And eventually, as they become more familiar with the pristine state of mind, they gradually realize more and more that their mental events are just illusions.

These two different experiences of realization—gradual and sudden—occur according to the individual's capacity and the proper conditions.

A CURE-ALL

When we see that all problems come from mental events, then we know that we can solve our problems by learning how to manage mental events through Pristine Mind meditation. This technique is in truth a panacea with the power to cure all mental and emotional suffering. It heals all of the mental and emotional turbulence that emanates from our misperceptions of the nature of our mind. If we are depressed, then what do we do? If we are not in a good mood, then what do we do? If we are in a relationship that is not going well, then what do we do? If we have anxiety and stress, then what do we do? If we are discontent or upset, then what do we do? What we need to do in all of these cases is rest in the present moment, maintain our Pristine Mind, and know that mental events are transitory and illusory. If we do that, any kind of disturbance and agitation will subside. Meditation with an understanding of these teachings enables us to do that.

When we are in Pristine Mind, the world around us may be chaotic or full of difficulties, but our own mind is clear and we can deal effectively with what happens, with love, compassion, joy, and impartiality. In Pristine Mind, our consciousness takes a journey without any burden of mental events or ego, aware of itself but connected with everything. Both positive and negative experiences, both significant and trivial circumstances, are components of our realization. We can go to the movies, eat well, deal with unfortunate events, and get new shoes with realization because the mind has been totally transformed. We can have both enlightenment and entertainment. There's no need to reject either one.

Once we perceive that our mind is innately pristine, we understand that our mental and emotional comfort is not dependent on circumstances, as in "Oh, I have a nice boyfriend, therefore I am content," or "I have a good job, therefore my mind is at peace." We are not constantly relying on circumstances. The capacity for unconditional happiness is built into our Pristine Mind. A deep and abiding sense of mental and emotional well-being comes with realization. When we recognize and experience Pristine Mind, healing comes from within, from inside our own consciousness, inside our own mind. Our Pristine Mind can never be taken from us. It is who we really are.

True Human Experience

Connecting to Pristine Mind is not a moment of bliss in which we glimpse some spiritual dimension temporarily. It is a real perception, a tangible experience that we can have like any other familiar experience. It is a real human experience, not a hallucinatory vision, an otherworldly mystical experience, or an altered state. It's not that one moment we are connecting ourselves to some magical place, and then disconnecting from it when we turn around to cook dinner or do the dishes. It is not as if we were plugging our meditation into the power outlet and then, after unplugging it, we revert to our distorted perspectives the rest of the time. It is a normal human experience, not a separate aspect of our life. With practice, Pristine Mind becomes second nature—in the way we make day-to-day choices, in the kitchen, at the office, or even in bed.

Sometimes people will say things like "Today I had a very spiritual experience" or "Ten years ago I had a life-changing spiritual moment," such as a vision of a divine being or a feeling of "oneness" with the universe. However, if afterward there is no real change happening in their life or their perception, moments of positive mental events like these are merely passing events. If we are not gaining permanent mental and emotional freedom, it is not true realization.

If Pristine Mind were just a temporary altered state of consciousness, or an experience of some other dimension, then it would bring about no change in our real life. Years could go by and we would still be under the same influence of our ordinary mind. Our perception would be the same, our habits would be the same, and everything would remain the same. There would be no transformation. There would be no real discovery.

But once we realize the nature of our mind, once we experience it directly, our perception shifts. We *do* change; we *do* become different than we were before. That's because it is a real experience. When we really do change, our attitude shifts. Our new perception becomes our reality. It is a transformation based on direct real personal experience.

How long does this transformation last? That depends on the individual. Some people are very familiar with the pristine state of mind. They just become one with that perception. They never forget it. But other people do not get really familiar with it. They may have just glimpsed it once and then never again paid attention to it. They may forget the perception and get caught up in their mental events again.

Beginners may forget it easily, but someone who accesses and remains in Pristine Mind regularly never forgets. They always experience Pristine Mind.

PART THREE

Meditation: The Journey Deeper into Pristine Mind

Perceiving who you really are is realization.
Abiding in who you really are is meditation.
—Mipham Rinpoche

10. Going Beyond Mindfulness

IN PART ONE, I addressed how our fundamental nature is pristine, but it is obscured by the experiences of our ordinary mind—our thoughts, emotions, belief systems, and ideas making up the mental events that form our concept of who we are. We are stuck in our mental events and develop ego, an unhealthy sense of self that obstructs us from the true core of our existence. We have lost touch with our Pristine Mind.

In part two, I explained how, through Pristine Mind meditation, we can directly perceive, experientially, the pristine nature of our mind. We developed our understanding of three fundamental realizations of Pristine Mind: who we really are—our Pristine Mind; who we are not—our ordinary mind filled with transitory mental events; and the illusory nature of our mental events.

Now that we have an understanding of Pristine Mind and an experience of the true nature of our reality, it is time to journey more deeply into it, to become really familiar with Pristine Mind and the vast, profound experience of the pristine nature of our mind. This is the subject of part three.

MINDFULNESS MEDITATION

First we must calm and stabilize the mind.

Initially, the winds of mental events blow through our minds incessantly with such strength that our minds are taken everywhere and anywhere by those rough winds. Before we can access Pristine Mind, we must quiet these gusty winds of thoughts and emotions. The technique for calming and stabilizing the mind is called calm abiding meditation, known popularly as mindfulness meditation.

The Buddha taught mindfulness meditation as a technique for beginners. It is a meditation practice that calms the mind by focusing on an object and abiding in the present moment. It is not the same as Pristine Mind meditation, but it lays a foundation for Pristine Mind meditation.

There are many forms of mindfulness meditation. One common method is to concentrate on the breath. To begin, sit down comfortably and relax your body, speech, and mind—this is the way we start any form of meditation. Then focus your attention on the sensation of inhalation and exhalation. When you inhale, focus on the sensation of inhaling. Do not focus on any other object or events of mind. When you exhale, focus on the sensation of exhaling and nothing else.

After ten or twenty minutes of continuously focusing on the present moment of the breath, the powerful inner winds that drive our mind in its chaotic activity soften, and the frequency and intensity of our thoughts and emotions decrease. Our mental events, while still present, slow down and are less all-consuming. Gradually, we are able to abide quite naturally in that more relaxed and stable condition. We become more present. This is the experience of calm abiding, which is the goal of mindfulness meditation.

Another, similar technique for mindfulness meditation is *counting* the breath. When we inhale, we silently count "one." When we exhale, we silently count "two." When we inhale again, we count "three." When we exhale, we count "four." We continue counting our breaths up to fifty or one hundred, or to whatever number we like, and then we start over again. If we lose track, we start again from the beginning or wherever we like. When we focus on counting the breath, our mind is focused on a single object and other mental events fall away. Our mind becomes more and more still.

Both of these methods, with practice, succeed in calming the mind and reducing the distorting mental events of our ordinary mind. As you will see, when your mind is fully focused on the breath as the object, other mental events have no opportunity to arise, and thus the mind is less vulnerable to the willy-nilly tendencies of the mind when it is left without a focus. Jealous thoughts, for example, cannot take hold in our mind because they need an object of jealousy. In the same way, unhappy thoughts cannot survive because they need an object of unhappiness if they are to flourish. All our mental disturbances in this concentrated state subside because we do not focus on the things that stir these emotions. When we remain with our mind concentrated on one thing, such as the breath, we experience our mind slowly becoming calmer and clearer.

Another technique for mindfulness meditation is to focus on a physical object, such as a flower, an image, or a letter. For example the letter *A*, *B*, or *C* can be used. The Tibetan letter *Ah* (ཨ) is traditionally used as an object of attention for this type of meditation. By remaining focused on the object, we do not let our attention go to anything else and do not let our thoughts move in any other direction. If we start having a thought that distracts us from the object, we just gently bring our attention back to the object, because if we follow the first thought, then another will come, then another, and we will completely forget about the object of our meditation. When the thought comes, we just recognize this fact and bring the mind back to the object.

With any of these techniques, we achieve the same goal: our mind slowly becomes more present and less distracted or obscured by mental events. We then have greater control over our mind. Without meditation, our mind is scattered and lacks sufficient discipline. It is very difficult to function truly effectively with this kind of disorderly mind no matter how hard we struggle. The chaotic functioning of our mind leads us to confused, ineffectual, and unhappy states of mind.

You will gradually begin to notice as you meditate more and more that anytime you are angry, unhappy, stressed, fearful, upset, or jealous, it is almost always because your mind is scattered, wild, and driven by impulses. As these mental events snowball, all kinds of information swirl around and all kinds of emotions are triggered. Patterns emerge and create repetitive tendencies based on what are really just disorganized activities of our minds. Thousands of emotions, hundreds of beliefs, millions of thoughts, emerge because our minds stray from the present moment. In this interior environment, it is almost impossible to find any calm, relaxation, joy, or clarity. Everything is chaotic. Most important, these mental activities, accumulations of thoughts and emotions, and habits cloud over the calm, tranquil state that we access in mindfulness meditation.

Mindfulness meditation techniques provide the antidote for this disorderly state of mind. If we do one of these forms of mindfulness meditation for ten, twenty, or thirty minutes every day, the mind soon becomes much calmer. For those who want to study these techniques further, many websites, books, and other sources of information are available. For our purposes here, however, it is simply important to understand that mindfulness meditation is a preparatory step in beginning to uncover our Pristine Mind through Pristine Mind meditation. As valuable as these techniques of calm abiding are, they stop short of the wonderful enlightened experience that is the Pristine Mind experience.

We progress from mindfulness to Pristine Mind meditation once our mind has calmed down. We no longer focus on our breath or any other object. All techniques of attention and focus on any object eventually dissolve, and we just rest in Pristine Mind.

To summarize, in the beginning we use a technique with an object, and then, after our mind is calmed and able to remain fixed on the object without distraction, we let go of the technique. Over time, as our mind becomes naturally calmer, we will need less mindfulness meditation before we switch to the unique features of Pristine Mind meditation.

In the famous work known in the West as *The Tibetan Book of the Dead*, Guru Rinpoche Padmasambhava gives lengthy, clear instructions about how we first practice mindfulness meditation to calm the mind, and then embark on Pristine Mind meditation. This process, originally introduced by the Buddha, is a tradition over twenty-five hundred years old and used over many generations to lead countless beings to enlightenment. First calm the mind with focus on the breath or another object; then, once the mind is calm, relaxed, and stable, move into the objectless meditation of Pristine Mind.

Is this two-step process the only way to embark on the Pristine Mind practice? Actually, you can follow this two-step process, or you can go directly to Pristine Mind meditation. Mipham Rinpoche tells us that in a world filled with so much stress, fear, and anxiety, mindfulness techniques such as focusing on the breath may not be effective in calming the mind. Instead, you can start directly with Pristine Mind meditation and get the benefits of both. As Mipham Rinpoche states:

> When you practice meditation, you can accomplish it by focusing
>   your attention on an external material object;
> You can concentrate attention on the sensation of breath;
> Or you can focus on symbols, letters, and the like.
> As you become accustomed to this process, you accomplish your
>   meditation.
> But in this time of agitated minds and rough emotions—
> Where frequent, intense stress constantly rattles like an aggressive
>   snake about to strike—

Even if you try to halt your thoughts, the effect is greater chaos.
Then you may become discouraged and give up your meditation.
When you settle into the unfabricated mind in its own true
    condition,
You become aware of it and continuously abide in this awareness.
Then even the storm of emotional disturbance does not disrupt
    you, and you don't follow it.
The nature of mind, like the sky, goes from clear to clearest.
Thoughts and emotions, like wind, go from calm to calmest.
Then the lake of your awareness becomes undisturbed, clear, and
    pristine.
You realize all qualities of the union of calm-abiding meditation
    and Pristine Mind meditation.

THE PURPOSE OF PRISTINE MIND MEDITATION

What distinguishes Pristine Mind meditation from other kinds of meditation? Unlike other practices, in Pristine Mind meditation, we do not
focus on any object. We do not focus on the breath or any other kind of
external condition or aid. Instead, we connect with the deeper part of
ourselves beyond mental events. We experience our true, flawless mind
without any distortions and see that it is a state that is always there. With
meditation practice, we gradually realize in a very deep and compelling
way that the mind is innately pristine, and we are able to more readily
develop the capacity to remain in that pristine state.

In fact, staying in Pristine Mind without any other conditions, without
any object or aid, is the actual Pristine Mind meditation. It is objectless
meditation. The more we remain in Pristine Mind meditation, the more
our Pristine Mind awakens and our experience of Pristine Mind expands
and deepens, both during the meditation session and afterward, in daily
life. Gradually, with more and more practice, as our experience of Pristine
Mind widens and deepens, the difference between our experience in meditation and our experience when we are not in meditation dissolves, and we
live more fully in the state of Pristine Mind.

This meditative experience expands into all other areas of our life. It
may not happen right away, but gradually the experience of Pristine Mind
infuses everything. Once we have allowed the obscurations created by our

ordinary mind to dissipate, we directly experience who we really, naturally are.

When we begin Pristine Mind practice, we use the four-step technique given to us by Guru Rinpoche Padmasambhava. Our practice with this technique is used to attain the three aspects of realization discussed in part two. We commonly refer to this as Pristine Mind meditation. Once our realization has taken firm root in our minds, then we abide in Pristine Mind; this *abiding* is the true Pristine Mind meditation.

Recognizing who we really are is realization. Abiding in our awareness of who we really are, maintaining that experience, is meditation. In Pristine Mind meditation, realization and meditation go together. As Mipham Rinpoche says, "Realization is like your eyes—they let you see who you really are; and meditation is like your legs—they get you from your realization to your ultimate awakening." Together, realization and meditation are the journey into enlightenment.

The goal is ultimately to become free from all mental events, including all negative emotions, distortions, and pollutions of mind, and to awaken our innermost essence, our natural state of mind—and, in doing so, to uncover enlightenment.

When our awareness becomes completely pristine, then our mental events no longer have the power to divert us from that vivid, clear, flawless state. When we reach that point, there is no anxiety, suffering, or fear in our minds. Those former mental tendencies simply have no more strength. That is the goal of Pristine Mind meditation: to achieve the completely pristine state of mind.

Now I would like to point out a common misperception about the meditation process. While writing this book, I was also taking English lessons. One day my tutor inquired about my occupation, and I told her I was a meditation teacher. She asked, "When you meditate, isn't it hard to stay awake when you are told to relax with your eyes closed?" I replied, "When we meditate, we don't close our eyes. We stay alert." This was quite a revelation for her. She was surprised because her idea was that meditation is a form of relaxation, in which we simply close our eyes and feel peaceful. While this may feel good or even have some health benefits, it is not what we are talking about, and it will not lead to the experience of Pristine Mind. Some forms of meditation are intended merely to relax the mind and reduce stress, but the forms of meditation taught by the Buddha are much more than that.

True meditation is not a temporary rest. When we are meditating only to pursue momentary peace, it is not a life-changing practice. It is really not much more than a good nap. When we talk about Pristine Mind meditation, it is much more than a nap. It is designed to access our mind in a way that transforms all areas of our life. When done properly, real meditation leads to unconditional happiness—a completely flawless and pristine state of mind.

11. GUIDED MEDITATION
The Experience of Pristine Mind

IN PART TWO, we went through a guided Pristine Mind meditation for the purpose of realization—to realize that Pristine Mind is the true nature of our mind, that ordinary mind is not who we really are, and that mental events have no objective reality of their own. Now we will engage in a second guided meditation—to journey deeper and deeper into Pristine Mind in order to experience its great benefits.

Each time we meditate, whether for realizing Pristine Mind or journeying deeper into Pristine Mind, we need to follow the same techniques. When we first *realize* our true nature, we use these techniques, and when we are *abiding* in our true nature, we also use these techniques. Whether we are just entering meditation or pursuing the experience of Pristine Mind all the way through to enlightenment, we must use the same four instructions that follow below.

In preparation, sit anywhere comfortable, such as a cushion or a chair, and relax your body. As mentioned earlier, this is always the first step to meditation. It does not matter where you sit, as long as you are comfortable. Relax your body. Make sure that there are no uncomfortable sensations or tensions in your body. Keep your eyes open. Silence your voice. Rest your speech, let yourself be quiet, and breathe in a very natural and relaxed way.

"Relaxing" does not mean we go limp and drowsy. Instead, our body and mind are alert and awake. We are relaxing from stress but not dulling ourselves or abandoning our awareness and succumbing to sleepiness or mindless daydreams. According to a well-known saying of the Buddha, we should be neither too taut nor too loose, like the well-tuned strings of a musical instrument. We are actively focused and alert. We are even enthusiastic about what we are doing.

While we remain alert, we allow our mind to be mentally, emotionally, and spiritually calm. We let go of any internal chatter by allowing all mental and emotional dialogue to subside. We do not try to engage in any thoughts or emotions. We just abide in alert awareness; we are conscious of our awareness. This is the preparation that we need for the true experience of meditation.

To continue to uncover our pristine, clear, calm state of mind, we need to orient our meditation around the four steps introduced by Guru Rinpoche Padmasambhava.

First, Guru Rinpoche Padmasambhava says, *Don't follow the past.*

We should not begin to wander in the direction of memories, thoughts, emotions, and images associated with the past. Instead, bring your mind into the present. The more easily and fully we arrive at the present moment, the more of our meditation time can be spent in the experience of Pristine Mind. Our ordinary mind makes it very difficult to stay in the present moment. One way it does this is by taking us back to the past. When we are fully in the present, we are prepared to journey into Pristine Mind.

Second, Guru Rinpoche says, *Don't anticipate the future.*

Do not let your mind begin to wander in the direction of future concerns and plans. If it does go in that direction, simply return to the present moment. We need not be concerned about anything in the future right now because at this moment, we are doing meditation. Meditation takes place in the present moment where Pristine Mind is experienced.

If we follow these first two steps, our mind is no longer caught up in the past or in the future. Most mental events, most negative thoughts and emotions, most things that disturb us, most unhappiness and sadness, come from focusing on the past or future. To clear these mental events before they even start, we need to release our focus on the past and future during meditation. We just bring our mind into the present moment.

The third step, Guru Rinpoche says, is, *Remain in the present moment.*

Just be present. Remain fully and vividly present.

Being present is an active process. It is a journey into an increased awareness of the present. We are not preoccupied with the past or the future because they take us away from this active focus on our own present awareness. We actively participate in that journey by focusing on our actual present awareness itself, all the while staying awake and aware. When we do that more and more successfully over a sufficient period of time, we begin to connect with our Pristine Mind, which is inherently present, here and now. This is not a passive experience in which we let our mind either lapse into dullness or run amok with thoughts and feelings. It is something we energetically pursue with great motivation and enthusiasm.

The fourth and final step in Guru Rinpoche's instructions is, *Leave your mind alone.*

Once we are fully present, what do we do with our mind? There is nothing to do with it. Just leave your mind alone. We continue to remain in the present moment, as we have described above. Be present and leave your mind alone without fabricating, without elaborating in any way; simply remain in that state. Just as we can leave our hand alone, we can leave our mind alone. If we leave our hand alone, we are not shaking it, making gestures, twiddling our thumbs, or lifting a cup. Leaving our hand alone means not doing anything with it. Just leave it there. Similarly, leaving our mind alone is not engaging in thoughts, emotions, memories, or future plans. Just leave it there so that we can be in the meditation experience.

After we follow these steps for five minutes or so, then true Pristine Mind meditation experience can begin. Once we have consciously remained in the present moment and left our mind alone for a few minutes, our mental events, our internal dialogue, our thoughts and emotions, all slowly subside. They subside because they cannot continue when we leave our mind alone. Mental events need an object to survive; the more we are present, the more our mental events subside. We have fewer and fewer overpowering mental events and swirling, stormy emotions. When we are fully present, when we completely leave our mind alone, all mental events subside.

When our mental events subside, what is left? What remains when emotions, thoughts, and belief systems dissolve? What is left is pure consciousness, pure awareness, Pristine Mind without layers, without distortions, and without obscurations. There is no mental or emotional pollution in that moment because it all subsides during each moment that we spend in the natural state of mind. Pristine Mind surfaces, and we experience it directly.

Once we experience that pristine state of mind, we simply stay there. We become familiar with it and abide in it as much as we can. This is meditation. Other than being who we really are, being in our pristine state of mind, there is nothing to meditate "on." While our pristine fundamental consciousness is innately present, it is meditation that reveals it. It is our meditation that lets us become familiar with it, familiar enough that one day it will be the way we naturally are, even without meditation.

That's what meditation is: in meditation we are actually remaining in Pristine Mind; we are not meditating *on* anything. Once we are in Pristine Mind, we just remain in it and continue the journey. We continue to not get caught up in mental events, not get caught up in the past or future. We develop intimacy with our natural state of mind.

There are no thoughts or emotions or other mental events to entertain in this state. It is much more comfortable than our ordinary state of mind. There are no ups and downs, no mood swings, and no good or bad states. It is clear like the blue sky. It is not like taking a nap or resting temporarily to get away from the turbulence of ordinary mind. Meditation provides much, much more for those who understand it and practice it.

DRIVING THE PRISTINE MIND HIGHWAY

One time I was traveling from Boston to Montreal to teach, and we were using the GPS in the car. I remember the GPS saying, "Continue on highway 89 for 50 miles." To reach our destination, we had to continue on that highway. If we had gotten off the highway, we would have had to return to it in order to reach our destination.

In the same way, when we practice meditation for thirty or forty minutes, we are continuing on the Pristine Mind highway for that period of time. When we are meditating, our internal GPS is saying, "Continue in Pristine Mind for 30 minutes. Do not exit." If our thoughts arise and we follow them, that means we are exiting. If we exit accidentally, then we need to come back to that Pristine Mind highway and continue on our way, so that we do not become lost. Then, if we just remain there, journeying on that highway, we progress toward enlightenment. We simply move through an increasing awareness of our present awareness, experiencing our capacity to be aware. Do not worry if thoughts arise. Thoughts are like exit signs. We just need to be aware that we do not exit and get lost. We may pass many off-ramps, but as long as we do not take them, we are fine. If we are always attentive to the longer journey, then we are in a good place, even if thoughts do arise.

The further we drive on that Pristine Mind highway, the more the environment changes. That drive I took along the East Coast was beautiful.

As we passed through each landscape, a new and beautiful environment surrounded us. Similarly, when we are on the Pristine Mind highway, our view of the world around us becomes more and more beautiful. We pass all our old habits and belief systems and the residual debris of mind until the most majestic experiences become our way of perceiving the world.

LEAVE YOUR MIND ALONE

In his instructions for resting the mind, Guru Rinpoche Padmasambhava says, "Leave your mind alone." In meditation we should have no fabrications, no resistance, no wandering, and no concern. Just leave your mind to be the way mind is naturally—calm and clear like water.

When there is too much going on in our mind, when our mind is distracted, unhappy, or stressed, if we are moody or agitated, what we need to do is leave our mind alone. At those times our mind is like water that has dust and debris stirred up in it. We must let the dust and debris settle to return to the calm and tranquil state that is actually inherent to our natural condition. When we do, the agitation, despair, and fatigue evaporate like a mirage when we approach it.

How do we clarify murky water? We don't shake it. We don't stir it. The best way to clear the water is just to leave it alone. Let it settle, and the water will naturally clarify itself. The water slowly regains its transparency after all the dust settles.

In the same way, when our mind is cloudy, unhappy, or agitated, the best way to improve it is to leave it alone and let it settle. Once we return to the present moment, there are no more mental elaborations; there are no mental contrivances, no judgments of any kind. Once we just leave our mind alone, then all these distortions and agitations settle down and the mind slowly regains its calm, clear, boundless state. A happy, clear, open state comes to the surface.

Leave your mind alone. So often, we mess with our mind and let ourselves be swept away by its troubled states. That's why we are so stressed and fearful much of the time. The working of our ordinary mind, which we tend to take as a given, is the origin of so many of these feelings, the mental junk and garbage that we call suffering. It does not have to be that way. Pristine Mind meditation is the highway to the essence of our nature, which is pristine and changeless.

Sometimes we may think, "I'm not doing anything to make problems for myself. I'm just stressed out." We don't think *we* are contributing to the cause of these feelings. We think we are just unhappy, stressed, or angry. We believe we are innocent bystanders to our experience, but that is not true. The mind is constantly creating the very suffering that we think we have nothing to do with. We may be sitting on the couch, seemingly passive, but actively thinking, "He did this. She is doing that. I don't like any of it. How did this happen?" Internally, an enormous amount is happening. We are pondering so many situations and dwelling on so many problems. We think this is all an involuntary and inevitable response to life, but leaving our mind alone is really all we need to do to release all stresses and other mental agitations. We do not need any other antidote. We need nothing but our awareness of the present moment of our Pristine Mind.

What is most important to understand here is that any fixation, fretting, or lingering is a form of messing with our own mind. What we need to do is remain in the present moment and not manipulate our mind in any way. Then our mind naturally becomes more clear and relaxed without our having to do anything. This all happens automatically. Our mind naturally becomes clear and pristine—calm, clear, and boundless.

How do we treat our mind properly? "Leave your mind alone." All disturbances and agitations come from not leaving our mind alone. Therefore, the way to resolve these problems is to leave the mind alone. That is the most natural way to prevent disturbances in the mind.

Once the mind is able to remain calm, clear, and boundless, everything is fresh and new in our experience. When we remain in Pristine Mind, all forms we see, all sounds we hear, all tastes, all sensory experiences, take on that fresh, sublime quality. After we exercise or do yoga and take a shower, we feel relaxed yet awake. There is a feeling of being present. It is similar, but much more profound, when our mind remains in the pristine state. Everything is vivid, boundless, and clear. We are refreshed on every level. Thoughts, emotions, and habits get old. Beliefs get stale. But when we remain in Pristine Mind, everything we experience has that same new, fresh, energized quality.

When we remain in that clear state, there are no judgments, there are no labels, there is no place to create and focus on negative experiences. The only thing to do is to maintain present awareness. Then everything we experience takes on that tone.

Once we learn to remain in Pristine Mind in our meditation session, then that pristine quality extends to our whole experience, our whole world. Thus, the reason we meditate is not to experience Pristine Mind only during formal meditation, but to have that experience carry over after meditation. Our experience will gradually carry over so that at all times we can access that fresh, clear experience—even when we are not meditating.

AN EGO-FREE ZONE

The Pristine Mind experience is an ego-free zone. An ego-free zone means that ego, an unhealthy sense of self, is not involved. In all our daily activities, ego is always involved, but in Pristine Mind there is no ego. There are only four avenues through which ego can operate: emotions, habits, beliefs, and thoughts. But in the pristine state of mind, none of those things exist, so ego cannot survive there. Without ego, there is no low self-esteem, no puffed-up arrogance, no false sense of self, nor any other unhealthy sense of self. Pristine Mind is a very comfortable state because no uncomfortable sense of self exists. It is a tensionless state without self-consciousness.

When we are meditating, we remain in that ego-free zone without rigidity or tension. We feel buoyant and unbounded. Neither a superiority nor an inferiority complex can take control. We are in a state of real rest, both mentally and emotionally relaxed, because these tensions and unhealthy senses of self no longer operate in Pristine Mind.

In fact, as we eventually discover, ego does not even exist; it is just a misperception. Once we have realization and we meditate, we directly perceive the truth, and the misperception of ego cannot survive. When all mental events are gone, then what is left is who we really are, what we truly are. Mental events, like those that constitute our ego, are temporary, artificial experiences. But when those are done and gone, what remains is Pristine Mind.

As our meditation progresses, the unhealthy sense of self gradually disappears. All the extremes of a sense of self—from self-conceit to self-loathing—dissolve during meditation. When we are meditating, that sense of self fades away. When we are no longer meditating, it comes back again. But that changes as well over time, depending on how familiar we are with the nature of our mind. The more connected we are with Pristine Mind, then the more confident we feel in that state and the more we develop a healthy sense of self. With a truly healthy sense of self, we realize that even our sense of self is a mental projection. Our self-perception is flexible and fluid. Our confidence does not depend on a rigid sense of self.

CRUISING ALTITUDE

When we transcend mental events by practicing Pristine Mind meditation, it is like reaching cruising altitude in an airplane. There is no turbulence whatsoever in our mind. We are free from disturbance and distraction, flying in a pristine state, completely serene, tranquil, and majestic. We effortlessly maintain that pristine state that is who we really are when we are not distracted by mental events.

An airplane can sometimes smoothly cruise for hours in the sky. Similarly, we have that same kind of experience when we become proficient in our meditation. For twenty minutes there is no turbulence in our mind, there are no mental events. It is a completely boundless, buoyant, and fulfilling experience. That is what it is like to remain in our natural state, our Pristine Mind.

Remaining in our natural state, remaining present, is not a blank or vacant state of nothingness, nor is it dull. We do not shut down our senses. In fact, we have the opposite experience. When we rest in Pristine Mind, we are much clearer and more present than when we are dwelling on mental events. We feel vibrant.

It is when we are dwelling on mental events that we are not present. They distract us from any deep and vivid experience of the present moment. To some extent we ordinarily do not really know what is going on around us. But while we rest in the present moment, we are aware of everything that goes on in the space we are in. We are not caught up in those things; we are just aware of them.

Meditation is not a dull or trancelike state, not a blank or unconscious state, and it's definitely not sleep. These are the opposite of the meditation experience. Instead, in Pristine Mind meditation we feel the freedom to be in that moment, free from all entanglements of mind, free from all distortions, elaborations, and contrivances. It creates a very relaxed, open experience. We are more present and able to live very comfortably in the present moment.

Even if we do not seek enlightenment, if we just want to feel happiness and joy and connect well with other people, Pristine Mind meditation is the best method. To connect with ourselves comfortably, or connect with other people with compassion and ease, we must first clean up the distortions of our mind. This is the function of Pristine Mind meditation.

Meditation is the best way we can improve ourselves mentally, emotionally, and spiritually. If we want to enhance our life, there are many different ways we can try to do it, but the real miracle for transforming our life is meditation.

Without meditation, our mind is always in "ego mode," and it is never relaxed. If we want to have a beautiful and comfortable mind, if we want to present ourselves beautifully and comfortably to the rest of the world, we need to practice meditation. The more we remain in the meditation experience, the easier it is for us to connect with other people, and the more comfortable other people feel around us. The more disturbed our mind is, the more things we are worried about, the more we dwell on difficulties, then the more uncomfortable we become no matter what the circumstances. All of these problems that result from our undisciplined mental events can be remedied by meditating properly.

A Boundless Experience

In Pristine Mind meditation, there is nothing to meditate on. Simply allow your awareness to be present. Allow your awareness to be free. Notice your awareness.

The most important component of meditation is to get comfortable being in the present moment. We are not paying attention to the breath or sensations or any other object.

Do not make the scope of your meditation too narrow. Do not try to force your mind or your visual focus to stay in one spot or in one particular place. Physically we can be very still, but mentally we might be entirely lost. Our awareness itself is the critical thing we are trying to abide in and become familiar with. We are simply hanging out with our pristine awareness and getting to know it more and more.

After meditating properly for ten to twenty minutes, we feel the boundlessness of our mind, at which point we simply maintain that experience. We do nothing but remain there. When we look out across that meditation experience, there is nothing to focus on. Allow your awareness to remain naked and free. Maintaining that state is meditation. Become comfortable and familiar with that meditation. We are not forcefully trying to do something. If there is effort involved in meditation, then it is awkward and uncomfortable. This meditation should actually feel effortless. It is a relaxed yet alert experience, spending time with our pristine awareness.

After we gain some experience doing this meditation, time starts to go by very quickly whenever we are meditating. It flies by. It feels as if we can continue indefinitely and that we want to keep going. We feel like staying there and not coming back out of our meditation. In meditation, when we feel like we want to remain in meditation, it is extremely positive. When we get to that point, it is a very good sign.

12. Experiences and Obstacles in Meditation

In this chapter we'll continue to walk through the experience of the formal meditation session and look at what occurs—the good and bad experiences that arise—and I'll advise how to relate to those different experiences. What happens when you are remaining in Pristine Mind meditation? For example, during meditation, if you hear a noise, what should you do? If thoughts arise, what should you do? This is what we will address now.

Noise Passes through Your Awareness

There is a significant difference between the experience of Pristine Mind meditation and that of other forms of meditation, especially practices that focus on an object. If our meditation involves focusing on a single object, as in mindfulness meditation, then noises or other external distractions can take us away from that focus. But when our mind is not focused on any particular thing, then that noise just passes through our awareness without interrupting our meditation at all. When we try to hold our mind on one point by focusing on a particular object in meditation, then our awareness is not expansive but is limited to that one object. But when we are remaining in Pristine Mind and not holding our attention to any particular object, our awareness permeates the entire space we are in. All sound just passes through our awareness, but it does not capture our attention or limit our awareness. After a certain point, when we are remaining in Pristine Mind, sensory inputs from the external world do not affect us.

This may not happen immediately, but the more familiar you get with Pristine Mind meditation, the less you are distracted by noise and other outer stimuli. You may want to start your meditation practice by deliberately reducing exterior distractions. It can be helpful to meditate in a quiet place without the sounds of ringing phones, televisions, and outside traffic, construction, or other street noise. Even experienced meditators derive a great advantage from going into a formal solitary retreat where outside interference is minimized. But accomplished meditators are less affected by outside stimuli; with enough experience, it will not matter whether you are in the noisy city or the quiet countryside, because you will have developed stability in Pristine Mind.

In addition to receiving impressions from the external environment, meditators frequently feel inundated by thoughts. Just having thoughts is not a problem for Pristine Mind practitioners. It does not mean we are not good at meditation. Instead, it is following, interpreting, and judging our thoughts that are the problem. Having thoughts come up is normal. We are used to having thoughts arise all the time. Having thoughts is a natural tendency. When thoughts appear, do not worry. Simply don't follow, judge, or interpret them. If we just remain in pristine awareness when we have thoughts, our thoughts will naturally dissolve by themselves.

There is no effort required to do this. We are not trying to create any specific experience. All we are doing is remaining in that calm state of being present, noticing our awareness. There is no effort involved in trying to make anything happen. We are not meditating *on* that state; we are just *in* it. The more we engage in this meditation, the more we simply feel ourselves in that state. Then our ordinary mental events cannot pull us one way or another. They cannot move us from that state of pure awareness.

In a way, it is not quite accurate to use the word "meditation" in talking about Pristine Mind meditation, because "meditation" suggests an action—that is, trying to accomplish something. In any type of object-based meditation, we *are* trying to do something. For example, in meditation on the breath, the whole point is to focus on breathing. We can say we meditate on the breath because in that type of practice, we are focusing on the breath. But in Pristine Mind meditation, there is no action or effort involved, and we are not meditating or focusing on anything. We are simply abiding in our awareness. We do not move away from that awareness unless we let ourselves get caught up in mental events. If we notice a mental event, we just let it pass, and it will not disturb our awareness.

The more we have access to and remain in this pristine state of mind, the more our mind becomes free of mental events and mental pollution, and the more we have the wonderful, beautiful experience of the mind remaining in its natural state. We are not meditating on anything. Instead there is the state of Pristine Mind that we are in.

CALM AND CLEAR

We can think of the four steps that Guru Rinpoche Padmasambhava teaches us as constituting "meditation." But when we have followed that progression of four steps and we are in the pristine state, then we let go of all methods. We are no longer employing a technique at that point; we are just remaining in that state. It is no longer a technique; it is real meditation. Pristine Mind meditation.

Dzogchen Master Shabkar says:

> There is nothing to focus upon.
> Rest your mind in an astonished, spacious, boundless state.
> Release your mind into a wide-open expanse.
> Do not elaborate or contrive.
> Allow your awareness to abide nakedly.

Each day when we meditate, we should remember that what we are doing is remaining in that state. Remaining in that state is much more natural than trying to meditate on something. Even the body language associated with these different types of practices is very different. When we are meditating on an object, the body tends to stiffen as a result of our concentrated focus. When we are abiding in a pristine state, the body remains more relaxed and natural. We can see this directly.

As mentioned earlier, some meditators practice with eyes closed in order to encourage a feeling of peace and relaxation. In contrast, our goal in Pristine Mind meditation is not just to achieve a momentary feeling of peace or relaxation; it is to go beyond our mental events and access Pristine Mind. We perform Pristine Mind meditation with the eyes open so that there is a more alert and aware quality to the practice. In Dzogchen, this quality is often referred to as "naked awareness." It is the aware quality of the untainted state of mind that is the essence of our meditation journey. That aware quality is a natural part of us; we are not separate from it. It is not something we have achieved. It is something that we are. It is this we are referring to when we explain the importance of finding out who we truly are. We begin to see that this calm, clear mind is our most natural experience. It is our true identity.

Our awareness has no restrictions. There are no boundaries in our mind. There is no self-consciousness or hesitation in that moment. We feel very open, relaxed, and blissful because our agitations no longer feel like a part of who we are.

It is very important to understand that the more we do Pristine Mind meditation, the more our immediate experience is pristine, clear, calm, and boundless. Ultimately, we will experience that to be the main characteristic of our mind.

This does not mean that during our Pristine Mind meditation session, we are supposed to experience a feel-good, pleasurable quality, or great love or compassion. There are specific meditation techniques for generating compassion, devotion, and other positive mental qualities. However, during Pristine Mind meditation, we just leave our mind alone. We don't try to generate positive feelings, and we don't linger over them if they occur. Pleasurable feelings are distractions. Both positive and negative thoughts and feelings are distractions. Feelings of generosity, devotion, compassion, and love for others during Pristine Mind meditation are distractions. Even thinking about the Buddha is a distraction at that time. Both white clouds and dark clouds obscure the pure blue sky.

Of course, after a formal session of meditation is over, we need to interact with our thoughts, emotions, and feelings. Outside our meditation sessions, we need to deal with circumstances; we need to analyze and understand past events, and make plans for the future. And we can engage in other techniques to increase our positive qualities. But as we become more familiar with Pristine Mind in meditation, we find that after meditation, our thoughts naturally become more positive and we have more control over our thoughts and emotions. Our thoughts have less of a feeling of solidity, less of a sense of concrete, unchanging reality. Our world becomes more malleable. We retain a boundless, clear quality in our mind in which compassion, love, and other positive qualities can thrive. Our feelings are less and less dependent on external conditions. Increasingly, we are gradually integrating meditation with daily life.

If we do not know that our mind is naturally pristine, then any calm, clear, or positive experiences or any sense of well-being we have are only temporary. So long as we still identify our self as the fundamentally negative, restless, or agitated ordinary mind, then our calmness or clarity is only momentary. We feel calm or clear for a few moments and then it disappears because we still identify that polluted, ordinary mind as who we are. Whatever calmness, clarity, spaciousness, tranquillity, or inner peace we experience are all temporary because we view those experiences as just moments arising against the backdrop of a complicated polluted mind. When we become more familiar with our Pristine Mind, then we know that who we really are is calm, clear, and boundless, and it is our negative experiences that become the momentary ones.

Just being told about these different experiences is of limited value. The only way to truly experience Pristine Mind is by meditating in Pristine Mind. Our understanding must be made real through meditation training and experience.

Hazy Mind

When people have anxiety, fear, anger, sorrow, and unhappiness, their mind is overcast. It is clouded over with thoughts. In that kind of cloudy mind, it is easy to get upset, to develop anxiety, to become unhappy. In a mind that has been habitually distorted and cloudy for a long time, reactions are triggered very easily. The disturbed mind feels volatile and is therefore fundamentally unreliable.

When one's mind is more open and clear, however, with fewer tendencies toward mental events, we say that it is more awakened or more pristine. In that state, anxiety, anger, or other negative reactions are not triggered as easily. Those types of reactions simply do not happen so readily, because the mind has greater stability.

If our mind is like a clear blue sky, it is less likely that it will be drenched by stormy emotions. If there are no thick clouds in our mind, if our mind is just a little bit cloudy, that is not an insurmountable problem. There may be a few clouds, but it does not rain. But if our mind is completely overcast, it rains very easily. Some people's minds are thickly overcast. Some people's minds even produce thunder and lightning. But a mildly hazy mind is something that can be worked through relatively easily with Pristine Mind meditation.

We can meditate with haziness and the meditation is still valuable; we can still make progress. The mind may be hazy at that moment, not completely pristine, but with meditation we are becoming increasingly familiar with what a clearer and clearer mind is. Our mind may still be hazy with mental events. But even when there are some clouds, we can still see the blue sky, at least to some extent.

When our mind is hazy, even though all mental events may not be completely gone, we can still access our Pristine Mind to some degree. So remember, when we meditate as a beginner, if our mind is hazy it is still fine. In this hazy state, thoughts and emotions do not overwhelm us. While we cannot meditate effectively with a completely overcast mind, very, very few meditators practicing Pristine Mind meditation have a completely pristine state of mind at first. Most have a hazy mind. Still, we learn that the mind is pristine innately, and we have a glimpse of that pristine experience. We have a view of that state through a thinning layer of clouds of thoughts and emotions. Eventually those clouds burn off. Slowly our mental events become less dominant and our hazy mind becomes a flawless Pristine Mind.

Pristine Mind meditation will even benefit a person with a mind full of thunder, lightning, and stormy weather. With diligent practice, the mental weather can calm down, going from stormy to overcast, from overcast to slightly cloudy, and ultimately, from hazy to flawlessly pristine.

Do Not Linger Over Mental Events

We do not need to have a completely pristine state of mind during meditation. Our mind may not always be like a completely blue sky. Do not worry. Until we reach completely perfect enlightenment, there are always some clouds in our minds. Even when our mind is remaining relatively pristine in meditation, some mental events still pass through. But having mental events occur is not a problem. For beginning meditation practitioners it is normal for thoughts to occur. You may think as you meditate, "I have so many thoughts. Meditation is not working." But, as we have said, having thoughts is not really a problem or an indication that meditation is not working. We are not trying to stop thoughts in our meditation. Rest assured, no matter how hard you try, they will not stop! They occur naturally. What we need to do is not follow the mental events that occur and not get caught up in them. If we pursue our thoughts and emotions, or get embroiled in them, then they become an obstacle and we will lose our meditation. As long as we don't get involved in our mental events, even if we have some thoughts here or there, we are still meditating well. The most we can do, and really all we need to do, is remain in Pristine Mind and leave our mind alone.

When you find yourself following your thoughts, simply come back to your pristine state of mind. No one can stop thinking all at once. We only need to be concerned if we get so caught up in a stream of thoughts, with one thought leading to another thought, that we lose track of Pristine Mind and become stuck in mental events.

We may get involved in thoughts from time to time; it is not a big problem. We simply need to return our mind to its naturally pristine state. With time, if we do this, our meditation will gradually improve, and eventually we will succeed in maintaining our mind in its pristine state despite the occasional passage of thoughts.

It is important for the beginner to realize that being in the pristine state of mind does not mean that we lose our awareness of sounds or other sensations. We may be meditating together with a group of people. When we rest in Pristine Mind and someone in the room coughs, for example, we are not oblivious to it. We hear the sound of a cough and we might even say to ourselves, "Oh, someone coughed." But if we let that thought go and continue to remain in Pristine Mind, our meditation is progressing well. That event passes and is gone.

But if we think, "Did somebody cough? Who was it that coughed? Oh, it was him. Why would he cough so loudly? I wonder what's wrong with him?" then we have lost Pristine Mind; we are caught up in a chain of mental events. That does not mean that we cannot acknowledge the bare fact that somebody made a noise. We are not oblivious to such things while remaining in Pristine Mind. We just do not get involved in any further interpretation of that experience. We hear it and acknowledge that the sound happens, but then we just remain in Pristine Mind without having to interpret or play out a story line about it. There is a huge difference between just hearing the sound of somebody coughing and playing out a whole stream of thoughts about that sound.

OVERCOMING OBSTACLES IN MEDITATION

All of the obstacles that people encounter during their meditation sessions can be put into two categories: dullness and distraction. You experience dullness when you are too focused inwardly and your mind gets sleepy, drowsy, and unclear. If you feel drowsy during meditation, you may get absorbed into the drowsiness and then get still drowsier or fall asleep. When that happens, you need to shift your gaze upward and make your mind more alert. You can drink some water or splash cold water on your neck or face, or go outside to refresh yourself. You need to wake yourself up and continue meditating. If you struggle with this, open your eyes a little wider. Increase your alertness so that your awareness does not feel clouded by the film of drowsiness. Just restore an awakened state and then remain in Pristine Mind. This will combat the dullness, drowsiness, and sleepiness that can sometimes be a pitfall in meditation.

The other major obstacle during meditation is distraction. Sometimes the mind is too wild. It is all over the place and cannot remain present. It follows after any sounds or sensations. It is overactive. It is as though hundreds of thoughts are buzzing around, overwhelming you, making it impossible to stay still within Pristine Mind. Your mind is overcome with restless energy. When that happens, gaze down past the end of your nose. Look downward and have your eyes less widely open. They should not be entirely closed, just not as widely open. Then you can focus a little bit deeper within and simply rest. This can help your mind stay calm and relaxed.

Initially, if there is a distracting sound, it is normal to be pulled in the direction of that noise. That happens to everybody and you should not be disappointed or feel as if you have failed at meditation. Your meditation experience is not yet like the Buddha's. You are not highly realized yet, so your mind will react to and follow in the direction of that sound.

Whatever sensations arise—the sight of moving shapes or blinking lights, changes in temperature, sounds from the street, an itch on your skin—your mind will go to them. All beginning meditation practitioners share these common experiences. It's not a bad sign; it is entirely normal. You should not feel concerned, discouraged, or upset. You need to learn not to get drawn too far away and not to get lost in the experiences of the five senses. Just come back to your Pristine Mind and simply leave your mind alone.

In addition to shifting your gaze to relieve dullness and distraction, you can also use the direction of your gaze to modulate your mental energy in meditation. Guru Rinpoche Padmasambhava says that if you get tired of gazing in one direction, you can shift your gaze up or down, or right or left, to help support the proper quality of awareness. This can also help if you feel bored or if you become tired of gazing with eyes fixed. It does not matter how you shift your gaze, as long as you continue to remain in Pristine Mind.

Don't Give Up

Pristine Mind meditation requires training. Suppose, for example, that we decide to take up hiking, an activity we have never done before. If we start off taking very long hikes in the mountains without prior practice and training, we should not be surprised that our legs hurt. We have not used them in this way before. We have never walked very much, so when we do walk a lot, all of a sudden our muscles tighten and we get sore. That is natural. But if we keep at it for a month, the muscle pains will go away because we will be trained to walk.

In the same way, when we first sit down to meditate, we might easily become discouraged because there are all these thoughts racing through our mind. But we should not give up for that reason. Just as in walking, if we have muscle pains at first and say, "Okay, I give up, I'm not a walker," then we will never get in shape—in the same way, when we sit down to meditate and we say, "Oh, I have too many thoughts; I guess I'm not a meditator," we will never experience our Pristine Mind or achieve unconditional happiness. We must practice to get beyond that initial experience of having so many thoughts. If we are diligent, the number of thoughts and other mental events will diminish. We must stick with it, however, and always return our mind to its pristine state as best we can. Increasingly we will be able to remain in that pristine state of mind.

Don't become easily discouraged. If you never try to go beyond that stage of initial discouragement because there are thoughts arising in your meditation, you are never going to have the true experiences of meditation. You need to go beyond that initial stage. You need to keep trying. If you keep making that effort to go beyond that initial discouragement, you will arrive at the experience of not getting caught up in your thoughts and mental events.

Sometimes you may even observe an increase in the frequency of thoughts. When that happens, don't get discouraged. My enlightened master Jigme Phuntsok Rinpoche says:

One sign that your meditation is beginning to be effective is that both subtle thoughts and obvious thoughts become more noticeable than before. This is not a bad sign; it's a good sign. When water rushes in a strong river current, you don't see the fish or rocks beneath the rapids. But when the current slows and the water becomes clear, then you can see the fish, the rocks, and everything below the surface distinctly. Similarly, if you never pay attention to your mind, and your thoughts and emotions are uncontrolled, you don't even know how many thoughts go by. But when your mind becomes more stable and calm, you begin to see your thoughts more clearly. Don't be discouraged. Take heart at this sign. Don't hold yourself too loosely or too tightly. Maintain your meditation in the right way without concern and gradually your meditation experience will increase and stabilize.

Remember: Do not follow the past. Do not anticipate the future. Remain in the present moment. Leave your mind alone. Those four simple, straightforward instructions give us a chance to go beyond our mental events and, eventually, to experience the natural state of mind.

At our beginners' level we need to meditate with diligence and enthusiasm because the winds of mental events are very strong. Once the winds of mental events die down and subside, meditation becomes effortless. Once our meditation gains momentum, once we get to cruising altitude, our meditation becomes natural. We are just *in* that state. We no longer have to meditate with effort. Really, it is not that difficult. When we are not lost in the past or future, when we are just there in Pristine Mind, that's the goal of meditation: to effortlessly abide in Pristine Mind in every moment.

One of the obstacles to beginners' progress in Pristine Mind meditation is the tendency to get lazy. We may find ourselves thinking, "This is too hard. I'm not really capable. I don't have enough time to get good at this. I'll get back to this some other time." The lack of obvious results from our efforts may lead to discouragement. This is just our ordinary mind at work.

To avoid and counteract this discouragement that can lead to laziness, we need to remember, contemplate, and ponder the four fundamental facts we discussed in part one—the rare and precious opportunity of human birth; the changeable nature of existence; the consequences of our actions;

and the discomforts of existence. We need to think about these things all the time, not just when we sit to meditate. And we need to integrate our understanding of these facts into our daily life, reminding ourselves that everything that occurs is an opportunity to choose between mental events and Pristine Mind. Contemplating these fundamental facts will help to overcome laziness and inspire our sincere and enthusiastic practice.

THE GROWING GAP BETWEEN MENTAL EVENTS

As we meditate regularly, over time, the gap or space between mental events becomes gradually wider. At first that gap is very small. The more we remain in that clear, present, boundless pristine state, the more that time between mental events expands. Eventually, it may last for twenty or thirty minutes, or even one hour. Then, for two hours after we meditate, there may be fewer mental events or no mental events, no heaviness in our mind. That means for those two hours we are in a blissful, relaxed, joyful state. As we get more and more familiar with our Pristine Mind and being in this really comfortable state without many mental events, we truly appreciate our meditation practice.

At first the heavier, denser, more frustrating and more rigid mental events dissolve. Then, gradually, the subtler thoughts and emotions disappear as well. The wider the gap between these mental events becomes, the more our inner nature, the pristine state of mind, who we really are, surfaces. This is the awakening and blossoming of our true nature.

The wider the gap between mental events becomes, the closer we are to enlightenment.

Creativity originates within this open gap. Once our mind is pristine, open, and boundless, we can express our originality spontaneously and naturally, unbound by our culture or belief systems. We can also deal with other aspects of life more easily because there is room in our mind and there are no internal mental conflicts. We can connect with people easily when we are that comfortable. Even if people we are talking with have a strong negative emotional reaction, we do not feel any need to react in kind. It is not because we are trying not to react, but because our mind is in a calm and pristine state. Often our calmer mind will make the other person feel calmer as well.

Once there is a significant gap between mental events, there is no obstacle to connecting with others. We are more open, more connected, more authentic. There are no elaborations or contrivances. What we say and do comes from who we really are, not who we pretend to be. As we remain in Pristine Mind for longer periods of time, for two or three or four hours, being connected to that state becomes our normal experience. The tendency to generate mental events is no longer a part of our mental and emotional experience. As our experience of Pristine Mind grows and expands, such tendencies shrink and fade. Mipham Rinpoche says, "If you practice even one week of meditation, the frequency of your mental and emotional impulses goes down." In the meditation retreats I have led for many years, I have witnessed the noticeable impact that even four or five days of meditation practice has had on my students' lives.

If we practice Pristine Mind meditation for just one month, we will notice even more improvement. Most of our stronger tendencies to create mental events and respond to them will subside significantly. We just need to understand how to get there. It's so simple: we just need to leave our mind alone. That is it. It is not a complicated solution.

Meditation is the best method for working with our mind. It is not a harsh treatment. Everything heals very naturally. And it is pleasurable, too. Meditation is like swimming. Some people enjoy swimming in the water; meditators enjoy swimming in Pristine Mind. Guru Rinpoche Padmasambhava says:

> Just like a great ocean undisturbed by wind, the nature of
>   reality is expansive and calm; abide without agitation
>   in the same way.
> Just like a bird that leaves no trace in its flight through the sky,
>   abide in your natural mind in the same way.

13. Beyond the Cushion

WE SIT QUIETLY while we are first training, but after we become more experienced and familiar with Pristine Mind, it doesn't matter what posture we are sitting in. It doesn't matter if we are sitting, walking, eating, or doing anything else. As long as we do not lose the present moment of Pristine Mind, we are meditating. As long as we leave our mind alone in Pristine Mind, we are meditating. That's the key. We can apply these instructions under any circumstances.

Guru Rinpoche Padmasambhava taught Yeshe Tsogyal, his principal disciple:

> If you don't know how to incorporate your spiritual practice into your daily life, then your meditation session just binds you. Generally, the least effective meditation holds the body and mind in a prison. That self-imposed restriction and pressure tie you up like a lasso.

Yeshe Tsogyal asked him: "Then how do you solve this problem?" Padmasambhava told her:

> Once you experience the ultimate nature of reality during meditation—abiding in that state that is completely free from all mental events—then you can take that experience with you after your meditation session. Whatever you do, you are not separated from that experience, whether you are walking, sleeping, resting, or sitting, at any time and during any activity. Then your meditation is free from the boundary of sessions.

PRISTINE MIND IN DAILY LIFE

There are only two choices for our mind. Either we are becoming caught up in our distorted mind or we are becoming familiar with our Pristine Mind. The terms *samsara* and *nirvana* refer to these choices. Samsara is becoming completely caught up in our mental events. Nirvana is becoming familiar with and aware of our Pristine Mind. The more aware of Pristine Mind we are, the more we remain in that state under any circumstance. Even when we are speaking or cooking, we can remain in Pristine Mind.

When we remain in Pristine Mind, things that once seemed boring or felt like drudgery now feel different. For example, many of us do not enjoy washing dishes. When we have become familiar with Pristine Mind and can stay in it, instead of feeling that we're performing a chore when we wash dishes, we can just abide in Pristine Mind.

As we become more familiar with meditation, it becomes second nature to us. Then washing the dishes passes by easily because we are not resisting it. It is that resistance that makes us feel the task is so unpleasant. For ten or fifteen minutes we must do something we do not enjoy. But it becomes easier when we remain in Pristine Mind, because we do not have that mind-set that says, "Oh, this is tedious. I can't stand washing dishes." Without that mind-set and resistance, time passes very easily and pleasantly. We are not just being mindful about what we are doing; we are in our Pristine Mind.

Once we know how to remain in a pristine state, we can remain in it under any circumstances—when we are washing the dishes, talking with someone, or going out to dinner. If we are out at dinner or anywhere else and we feel anxious or uncomfortable, if we are familiar with Pristine Mind and have cultivated our access to it through meditation, we can simply return to Pristine Mind and remain comfortable.

There is less cloudiness and less discomfort because, as we engage in conversation, we are not constantly sifting through an overload of mental clutter. Our now-clearer mind is not fending off a bombardment of competing thoughts. Communication is clearer because the thoughts that are useful to express are not jumbled together with the hazardous materials of emotions, mental events, projections, and distractions. Someone whose mind is overwhelmed by mental events is running several simultaneous conversations with his or her own thoughts. Not surprisingly, it is hard to maintain any truly meaningful dialogue with anyone else. But if we are on a "low-thought diet," then useful, intelligent, helpful thoughts are not obstructed at any moment; instead, they arise more freely. My enlightened master Jigme Phuntsok Rinpoche says:

> The five senses and consciousness are like the reflections of the stars
>   and the moon.
> Even though they reflect on the lake of clear, pristine awareness,
> The lake remains free of the waves of all mental events.
> This is the exceptional and effortless path of Dzogchen.

The meditator's mind remains calm and clear, like that lake; at the same time, the meditator sees, hears, and experiences the world clearly, and engages in any number of activities, without any ripples or waves of mental events. If you have had a taste of this experience, that is wonderful. If you have not yet tasted it, just continue practicing and eventually you will develop this taste. It does not fall within our ordinary experience; it is something extraordinary and wonderful. In my experience, it is the best way to truly bring unconditional happiness and fulfillment into our lives.

14. Receiving the Benefits of Meditation

THE WAY to break through the restless habits of the mind is through meditation. Meditation frees the mind from its compulsive tendency to engage, engage, engage. This brings tremendous liberation. Once we are free from that compulsion, whether we engage or we rest, we are comfortable. We do not need to always engage. Without engaging we can still find comfort. We can choose to engage comfortably when the time is right.

From Addiction to Contentment

So long as we are addicted to external conditions, when we engage with the world we feel good, but when we try to rest without external stimuli we can be lost, anxious, and confused. We do not know how to remain in connection with who we really are. This is why we compulsively engage in so many activities, one after another. With meditation, we break through our addictive habits. Then we can remain in touch with our true nature very comfortably, and we can engage as we need to engage, in a very healthy way. In that pristine state, we see everything more vividly than we do when our mind is stressed and agitated. We can appreciate the world of the senses much more when we remain comfortably in the natural state of mind.

When we are overwhelmed with stress and agitation, we cannot feel the beauty of the world through our senses the way we can when we are resting in Pristine Mind. The layers of agitation prevent us from seeing and experiencing the world with the vividness we experience in Pristine Mind. When our mental events are so active, we send out negative energy, and it bounces back at us in the form of our experience of the world. If we send negative energy, unhappiness, tension, and anger out to people, they pick up on it and they reflect it right back to us.

But when we remain in the pristine, genuine state of mind, then we send out positive, pleasant energy into the world and the world reflects it back in response. This is what happens when we learn how to rest in Pristine Mind for just five, ten, or twenty minutes a day.

With our mind in that beautiful, pristine state, very restful and relaxed, we can see and appreciate the entire external world, clearly with all our senses, without layers of agitation obscuring it. There is nothing between us and the universe. The universe's beautiful nature and the beautiful nature of our mind are one. There is no duality separating us from our experience.

When our meditation expands and we can stay immersed in a pristine state of mind for thirty or sixty minutes, the frequency of our habitual restlessness really slows down. When that happens, without our doing anything, we feel happiness. Pristine Mind meditation lets us be comfortable whether we are involved with our surroundings or not.

We need to find a way to rest in such a way that even without doing anything, we still feel comfortable, happy, and content. How do we get there? Through meditation. When we gain mental stability through meditation, then, without doing anything, we can find happiness and contentment.

I notice that the real benefit in my own meditation has been that my restless energy settles down. Once that restlessness settles down, we can enjoy the world of the senses, or enjoy remaining in the present moment without engaging. That is because we are in Pristine Mind.

UNDERSTANDING "THE VIEW"

Once we have really realized the nature of our Pristine Mind through meditation, we have a very different experience of our entire reality. Our attitude toward our mental events and toward ourselves, the way we relate to happiness and sorrow, is totally different than it was when we did not realize in a deep and meaningful way that our mind is pristine and before we began to meditate to experience that pristine state. With realization and meditation, even when we are not meditating, we will have a completely different understanding of our entire reality, an understanding that takes place on a very deep level.

Familiarizing ourselves with Pristine Mind through meditation creates the shift that brings the new perception. Someone with this type of perception is not like an ordinary person. Their mental, emotional, and spiritual experience is very different. When we have that perception it means we have what the Buddhist teachings often call "the view." If someone has the view, they hold the special perception that only high realization and meditation bring. It is a rich experience of Pristine Mind.

How can we tell if our meditation is working? If our mind reverts to being ordinary as soon as we stop meditating, and if we keep the same perception we had before we ever started meditation, then there is no progress, no improvement, no transformation. If we find there is no discernible difference between our attitude and the attitude of someone who does not meditate at all, then it is likely that our meditation is just serving as a temporary solution, a pleasant interlude in a still-troubled experience of the world. If we find this is the case, then we need to work more diligently on the four instructions described in our guided meditations—especially the instruction to leave our mind alone.

The success of our meditation is measured by how much our perspective improves throughout all aspects of our life. This attitude shift happens outside of meditation sessions, not just when we are sitting on a cushion. If there is no change in our perception, then it may be necessary to consult with a qualified teacher. If there is a significant change in our experience throughout our day-to-day life, even when we are not meditating, then meditation is having a real and positive impact. It is a sign that our meditation is achieving a beneficial result.

Fantastic Bodies and Difficult Minds

People care so much about the shape of their bodies that they exercise and go to great effort to make their bodies beautiful. But while they have fantastic bodies, they endure difficult minds.

Through movies, television, newspapers, magazines, and social media, modern culture bombards us with messages about how we should look. People feel compelled to go on the latest diets and work out to develop slim figures and gorgeous muscles, because the world tells them that it is important to be attractive if they want to be valued by others. But the world around us rarely tells us of the importance of having a beautiful mind, of mental and emotional well-being . Many people who have gorgeous physiques are celebrated in the media. But where are the people with gorgeous minds?

People can have perfect bodies and yet be mentally and emotionally distorted. Their minds are the opposite of relaxed. Even if we have a nice, healthy body, if we are mentally and emotionally polluted, we do not enjoy life. Something is missing. We have the physical side of the happiness coin, but the mental side of the coin is blank.

Mentally and emotionally we carry thick layers of habits, stress, fear, resistance, and worries. If we lack the beauty of good mental qualities, our physical body and mind are a painful contrast. We may see beautiful people on television appearing to be having fun, but if we could look inside their minds it might be a very different story.

When physical discipline and mental discipline are moving in opposite directions, it creates tremendous tension. But when all the physical, mental, and emotional components of our lives are aligned, it is a very beautiful, wonderful experience. Physically we need to exercise and eat right. But mentally, emotionally, and spiritually we need to train our mind with meditation to be prepared to deal with mental events. Then gradually the weight of mental and emotional distortions diminishes.

People are sometimes depressed, angry, and lack good relationships. If their minds feel overwhelmed with stress and unhappiness, of course they have a hard time relating to others; their minds are completely out of shape. They are just like that person who never exercises and is always eating junk food. Without meditation, our mind is easily controlled and dominated by the stresses and moods of mental events. The mental events have become so powerful that we are a slave to them. We have no power to get them to subside or disappear.

To reap the full benefits of meditation, I strongly recommend practicing at least a few times a week. If we do it regularly, like exercise, then it prevents mental events from controlling our mind. In our physical exercise, if we stop exercising for too long, we will get out of shape and will need to rebuild that momentum; but if we exercise regularly, we gain strength and improve our health.

It's very similar with meditation. If we never meditate, we are like someone who overeats and never exercises. Our mind is out of shape and very unhealthy. It can be hard to start directing the mind in a healthy way again. If we do not meditate regularly, our mind reverts to being polluted and distorted. Once it becomes completely distorted, then it can become very hard to start meditating again.

But if we practice meditation regularly and remain present in Pristine Mind, then we can break the chains of mental events. Each time we meditate, we have more access to that clear mind as we break through more mental events. If our mind is calm and relaxed, even if we are surrounded by many irritations, we will not have such an adverse reaction. We will have more patience and may even laugh and see the irony of what would otherwise be an irritating situation.

If we meditate regularly, our mind becomes more relaxed, calm, and clear. Then all positive qualities surface; it gives us a healthy, happy, more tolerant and enlightened mind.

APPLYING MEDITATION IN THE MIDST OF DIFFICULTIES

The time when we need to apply Pristine Mind meditation the most is when we are experiencing difficulty in our life, when the circumstances around us are at their poorest. In these times, too, it is possible to quiet our thoughts and have a Pristine Mind, even when we feel miserable. We can apply Pristine Mind meditation in the midst of difficulty, we can apply it while experiencing suffering and challenges, and we can apply it under any other circumstances.

The way to apply this practice at any time in your life, regardless of the circumstances, is to follow what Guru Rinpoche Padmasambhava says:

> Don't follow the past.
> Don't anticipate the future.
> Remain in the present moment.
> Leave your mind alone.

If we know how to access our Pristine Mind at any time, in any moment, including at times when we feel upset or the circumstances are difficult, then we have the ability to solve our problems and difficulties. If we remain present and meditate, then slowly our agitation fades away and dissolves, and our pristine clear state of mind comes to the surface. Whatever is bothering us—sadness, anger, obsession—slowly fades from our perception and dissolves as our Pristine Mind appears. And when we become accomplished meditators, we can take action at any time, we can cut through mental events—especially negative, uncomfortable, or hurt feelings—immediately, as soon as they appear, without having to stop and engage in formal meditation.

In the midst of very heavy life experiences, our mind may need to take more time to rest and settle down because there is so much distorted energy to dissolve. At the beginning it can be difficult because thoughts and feelings have their own attraction, pulling us in their direction. But as it becomes easier for us to apply meditation, the easier it is to dissolve even very strong emotions and misperceptions.

Once the agitation in our mind subsides, we can connect with everyone in the world because we are completely comfortable and totally relaxed.

THERE IS NO RESISTANCE IN THE PRESENT MOMENT

When we first start to meditate, each session may feel like an eternity, but eventually we notice that the time seems to pass much more quickly. This is a very good sign.

The reason time initially can seem to go on and on forever is because we are resisting the present moment when we sit down to meditate. We are trying to speed it up a bit. We think, "Let's get this over with. What time is it? How long has it been? How much longer? My knee hurts. I don't want to sit still anymore. I'm bored." The emotional, reactive mind is always fighting against the present moment and constantly resists it.

When we are in that boundless state of Pristine Mind, it reduces all this resistance to being in the present moment. Then the time passes quickly. The accompanying stress and discomfort created by our own resistance subsides. If we are thinking, "I can't wait for this to be finished; this is taking too long," it creates an anxious feeling and makes meditation feel like it takes forever. It's only due to that stress, that feeling of discomfort, that it feels like an exercise that seems to go on and on. But when we remain in the present moment in boundless Pristine Mind, there is no resistance. Since there is no resistance, there is no discomfort, anxiety, or tension. This allows time to pass by very quickly. An hour can pass, and yet it hardly feels like it has been any time at all because we have been very comfortable that entire time. We have been at ease with the silence, our self, and our mind. All of these are indications that our meditation is progressing well.

The Place and Time for Meditation

People often ask me exactly how long, down to the minute, they should practice meditation. In the same way that there is a certain amount of time we need to exercise in order for the physical benefits of the exercise to really begin, there is a certain amount of time we need to meditate to really benefit from it, particularly when we first start meditating. I recommend meditating at the beginning at least two or three times a week for twenty to thirty-five minutes each time, if possible. Although this may seem long at first, a shorter time is not really enough to get the full benefit from the meditation because it takes some time for the mind to settle down and to really begin to enter a natural state.

When we exercise, we need to warm up and gradually increase our heart rate until we are fully exercising. If we stop before we get to that level of exertion, we do not really get the full benefits of exercise. A person who exercises only fifteen minutes a day and does not increase the length of the exercise sessions or use heavier weights may reach a certain fitness level. This may be sufficient for physical fitness, but in the journey of Pristine Mind, there is no upper limit. If we only meditate for ten or fifteen minutes, that meditation doesn't have as big an impact on us as it does if we meditate longer. Our mental events are still very present. We may never get the most powerful benefit.

Of course, we get benefits from meditating even only ten or fifteen minutes—it reduces our focus on mental events, it boosts our level of vitality, and it increases our positive experiences. So while we can do meditation for however long we want, and no matter how long our session is, it will be better than not meditating at all, if we really want to get the most benefit from our meditation we should meditate for twenty to thirty-five minutes or more at a time.

I have heard some people say their meditation has not helped them. Sadly, I suspect that these practitioners may get close to the point where they can access Pristine Mind, but then stop before fully connecting to it. They never get past that initial phase.

But if we spend fifteen or twenty minutes following the instructions so that our mental events calm down, and then enter into and remain in that pristine state for another fifteen minutes, our practice will have a huge impact. Getting into the natural state takes time. Experienced meditators may enter into that state easily, but for others it takes time to get into it. We need to give ourselves enough time for our mind to settle down during each session so that we really get the benefits of meditation. That is why I suggest meditating for twenty to thirty-five minutes at a time in order to make sure we do actually abide in Pristine Mind.

These guidelines are mainly for beginners, less so for people who have already developed a strong meditation practice. As a beginner, it's critical to be realistic and discipline oneself to take the time necessary to actually settle down and enter into Pristine Mind, and then to remain in that state. That is how we become familiar with Pristine Mind, and it is essential to developing a genuine meditation practice. Only then will we truly get the benefits of meditation.

Aside from taking enough time to meditate regularly, it can help very much to practice in a group as well as by ourselves at home. Coming together to practice as a group is very helpful because then we motivate each other to practice more. It is like people going to the gym together or joining a yoga class to work out and practice together. To further our familiarity with Pristine Mind, we need opportunities to come together as a group and practice meditation.

Formal meditation is the regular time that we set aside to sit down on our chair, cushion, or mat, and develop our meditation. Beginners often ask *where* they should meditate. Many meditators find it helpful to have a specific space for meditation set up in their home, to be used only for that purpose, such as a separate room or the corner of a room. We can place there a small statue or painting of the Buddha or Padmasambhava, or any other object or artwork that supports our meditation. Our meditation shrine can thus serve to inspire us and to remind us of the need to practice regularly.

But in reality, all we truly need is a comfortable space. Once we have established our practice, then we can do it anywhere. We can do it in any place, during any activity, or under any type of circumstance.

DYING WITH PRISTINE MIND

Pristine Mind meditation must be applied throughout all phases of the living process—and that includes during our sleep and dreaming episodes and during the dying process. It can be applied at the moment of death, and applied in the states of consciousness that arise after we die. It can be applied to every moment that our consciousness experiences.

If we have stability in our meditation during this lifetime, we can also achieve stability at the moment of death. We can gain the strength not to become lost in hopes and fears and attachments at that critical time.

Guru Rinpoche Padmasambhava explains that after our body and mind become separated from each other upon dying, then we lose consciousness. Once we become completely unconscious, we have no awareness or mental activity. That is death.

When we awaken after this passing and regain consciousness, we are no longer in this realm and no longer have this body. We regain consciousness in another dimension. It is a dreamlike experience.

At that moment, if we do not recognize that everything is just a projection of our own mind, then we will become completely lost in the experiences that arise. As sounds, lights, and other experiences arise, our consciousness is like a feather in the wind, blown about by those experiences. If we have stability of Pristine Mind, however, during this lifetime, any after-death experiences that arise are all automatically interpreted correctly and we are not subjected to the painful distortions of a polluted mind.

At the moment of death, it is most important that we have a Pristine Mind and not a polluted mind; it is the best way to die. Someone who is familiar with Pristine Mind dies without fear, anxiety, or agitation. With that familiarity, at the very moment of death our consciousness is more vivid, clear, and brilliant. When we gain confidence in our practice, then we are already prepared for the moment of death.

"Hell" is having a polluted mind. When our mind is polluted, everything is polluted. Without our polluted perceptions, there is no hell.

Pristine Mind brings pristine experience. There is no heaven other than this state. Experiencing Pristine Mind is heaven because once our mind is pristine, we experience the state after death—the time between births—and our next life as well, as pristine. This is why it is especially important during this life that we detoxify our ordinary mind by accessing Pristine Mind. That is our greatest priority.

PART FOUR

A Good Heart: The Companion to Pristine Mind

May all beings have happiness and the causes of happiness.
May all beings be free from suffering and the causes of suffering.
May all beings never be separate from unconditional happiness,
where there is no suffering.
May all beings live in great impartiality, free from
attachment and aversion.

— The Four Boundless Attitudes to Cultivate a Good Heart

15. THREE PRINCIPLES
Realization, Meditation, and a Good Heart

A COMPLETE PATH to enlightenment relies on three principles: realization, meditation, and a good heart.

We have explored the first two principles of our journey to enlightenment: realization, which includes both a knowledge and experience of Pristine Mind and its characteristics; and meditation, which enables us to become more and more familiar with the state of Pristine Mind by abiding in Pristine Mind for longer and longer periods of time.

There is a third principle we must understand if our journey is to be successful and lead us to enlightenment, the permanent connectedness with our Pristine Mind: we must develop a "good heart."

We are told by our parents, teachers, and others that it is important to be a kind and loving person—to be kind-hearted. And, of course, it is. However, there is an aspect of this that may cause some to dismiss the importance of a good heart. When we are told to be kind and loving toward others—not to lie, cheat, steal, or harm others; to be faithful and responsible; and similar admonitions—these instructions are given to us as moral imperatives; if we do these things, we are good, and if we don't, we are either bad or we have some kind of mental impairment.

However, having a good heart is not just morally correct; it is also functionally relevant to our everyday life as well as our spiritual development. In other words, the moral dimension of having a good heart is not that crucial; instead, what's really important is that having a good heart has essential practical advantages for our lives. Having a good heart makes our lives happy, powerful, joyous, and harmonious. This is true whether or not we desire enlightenment. The role of a good heart should therefore not be equated with religious or social conventions of virtuous behavior.

Realization, meditation, and a good heart are the three principles that lead us along the path to enlightenment.

Having a good heart gives "lift" to our meditation practice. If we want to go beyond negative thoughts and emotions, and transform everything in our life positively, then we need to have a good heart. A good heart gives us mental and emotional strength. When we live with a good heart, our inner experience is lighter and more buoyant, making the path to enlightenment more traversable.

During meditation, our job is to go beyond all mental events, whether positive or negative. When we meditate, we don't get caught up in a sentiment of any kind, whether it's love, compassion, or other positive events, or anger, unhappiness, or other negative events. But at every other time, we need to cultivate the proper environment for meditation. We need to develop, enhance, and increase our positive mental events. Otherwise, our minds have no fertile ground for Pristine Mind to flourish.

We should also recognize that having a good heart is crucial for happiness and contentment. A good heart inevitably leads to harmony and joy, even for someone who has no particular desire for enlightenment. Whether you want to just have a good life or you want to attain ultimate enlightenment, you need to be on the road of the good heart. It's like driving on Highway 101 in California. You can start in San Francisco and get to San Jose. But if you keep going on the same highway, you can get all the way to Los Angeles.

OUR WORLD IS COLORED BY OUR MIND

We need to cultivate a good heart in a conscious way, because otherwise we see the world through the distorted lens of our ordinary mind. Our world is colored by our mind, so the qualities of our mind determine our perception of the world. If our mind leans toward the negative, then the world will appear negative. However, if our mind leans toward the positive, then the world will appear positive.

Our mind is like a movie projector. We begin with our inborn mental propensities. We unconsciously select from the myriad of opportunities that the external world gives us, to shape our inner reality. Then we project those selected images onto our experience of the world. If the projector has been filled with content such as fear, resentment, discomfort, self-centeredness, selfishness, discontent, or entitlement, then we project these mental images and patterns onto the external world, and we think the external world is causing us to feel that way. If we are self-absorbed, we then see the world as self-absorbed and we feel uncared for. In truth, however, it is our mind that is really in that state, not our external world.

If we project our image of the world through a filter of resentment, then what we see is imbued with resentment. Being with other people makes us feel and act disagreeable because we automatically feel the resentment that we ourselves project when we see others. As long as our mental projection machine is filled with negative content, then the presence of other people will make us uncomfortable in a manner consistent with what we project. This in turn becomes a self-fulfilling prophecy. If, for example, because of our sense of unfulfilled entitlement, we feel chronic resentment, then we will project that mind-set onto the world around us. People seem to resent us, and we never feel appreciated or satisfied by friends, family, or partners. When we greet the world with an inflated sense of entitlement, it is extremely hard for the world to meet our unrealistic expectations. We think it is the world that upsets us. In truth it is actually our own mind imposing its framework on the external reality in a manner that then creates the very expectations we brought to it.

In light of our ordinary mental propensities, how are we to go about having a good heart? There is a way. It starts with understanding that we are all the same. Everybody is just like us. We all want to be happy. This is the way to counteract our mind's negative propensities.

But what is a good heart, and how can we develop it to reach its highest potential?

Four Components of a Good Heart

A "good heart" is more than a single quality. There are four components or qualities of a good heart: love, compassion, joy, and impartiality. These are sometimes called the four boundless attitudes.

It's not as if we either have these four attitudes or we do not. There are varying degrees to which different people experience each of these attitudes. There are degrees of love, degrees of compassion, degrees of joy, and degrees of impartiality. The higher degree of each of these we have, the more it helps us and others, and the more selfless and genuine we become.

The best that humanity has to offer comes from these qualities of a good heart. Throughout history the most courageous, majestic people possessed these four components of a good heart. That is why they have had such a positive impact on the world.

It is not as if we have to develop a characteristic we do not possess naturally. We all already have these tendencies to some degree; all we must do is enhance them. The more we enhance our positive attitudes, the more happiness and harmony we experience.

So much of humanity's problems originate from our forgetting these four positive attitudes. Instead of remembering them and training our awareness on them, we let ourselves be controlled by negative tendencies like greed, anger, jealousy, resentment, and guilt. When we enhance these negative attitudes instead of those that comprise a good heart, we increase our unhappiness and disharmony. All conflicts, great or small, occur because these negative tendencies become overpowering. We do not recognize that with proper attention and training we can alter those painful and unpleasant feelings.

WE ARE ALL ON THE SAME FLIGHT

Wherever there is a mind, there are experiences. On a physical level we feel sensations, and on a mental level we feel emotions and have thoughts. That is how we all are. Every individual is the same in this regard. Any person who has feelings, emotions, and sensations also wishes for happiness and to have the conditions needed for happiness. And we all want to avoid suffering and the conditions that cause suffering. This is a universal truth.

A good heart originates from paying attention to and understanding other people's situations in life. It comes from recognizing what we all have in common. We realize that all those we see—including the old man, the small child, and the middle-aged woman—are exactly like us. They, too, just want to live happily in this world. When we ask ourselves what we desire, we see that fundamentally the answer is the same for all of us. We want happiness and we do not want to suffer. When we truly recognize the universality of these wishes, we then are able to want happiness for the old man, the small child, the middle-aged woman, and all other beings. We do not want them to suffer.

This is the origin of a good heart. The understanding of this most basic fact about our universal human wish is the perspective and attitude that we need to uncover our good heart—that aspect of our mind that is so important, not only for our progress toward enlightenment, but also for our everyday happiness. Indeed, without it there can be no progress.

When we are traveling in an airplane, all passengers on the plane share something in common. There may be a couple having a conversation, a grandmother reading a book, or a child sleeping. But if we look at all these people, what do they all want? Every one of them wants a pleasant, safe flight free from turbulence or disturbance. They all want to arrive safely at their destination. Every single person, individually and collectively, shares the common interest in arriving at their destination safely and comfortably. There is, even with these strangers, some sense of caring about each other and a feeling of being part of a larger group.

In the same way, we are born together in this world. We share this world, this environment, this country or this city, with everyone else who lives here. All of humanity wants to try to live in this world and to have happiness and the conditions for happiness. Everybody wants happiness. Nobody wants suffering or the conditions of suffering.

The more we reflect on this perspective on what other people want, the more we understand what motivates them. We see our common humanity.

The truth is that everybody is the same. Everybody is just like us. Why would we want happiness but other people not want it? Why would we want to avoid suffering but other people not want that? The world does not exist only for *me*. The world exists for all of us. This attitude is the source of a good heart. Once we understand this truth, then it slowly leads us to the thought that everyone should be treated well.

Then, with that perspective, whenever we meet another person, we see someone who wants to enjoy life and who does not want to be hurt or to suffer. Just as much as we want happiness, so do they. They do not appear so different from us. They do not feel like a stranger. There is no confusion and no uncertainty. We don't think, "Who is that person? Why is he here?" "What is her problem? What does she want from me?" "What are they doing in this world?" None of these suspicious and potentially resentful feelings arise. Instead, we are more likely to think, "They want to be happy, just like me." So why do anything to make them sad or angry? Why do anything to hurt them? It will just make them unhappy. We don't want harm for ourselves, so there's no reason to do something that will harm others.

In the same way, when we encounter our friends, family, or co-workers, if we have developed the perspective that they are just the same as us, then even if there is a conflict or disagreement, that perspective will totally change the way we deal with the conflict. The particular way we respond to the conflict may vary according to the circumstances, but the method we use will be based on trying to understand the other person rather than just trying to win the conflict. Even in conflict, if we have the perspective that the other person is just like us, then we perceive the other person differently, more reasonably, and as a result the other person has a more positive experience of us. This reduces the conflict. As we act more reasonably, the other person's attitude changes, and they act positively as well.

A good heart connects us positively with the world, with other people, our friends, our family, and the rest of humanity. If we want to have a connection with others, to enjoy a harmonious and genuine connection with the world, we need to have a good heart. Without a good heart we live in a world of separate individuals who are more like isolated scattered islands than a cohesive, interconnected city. A good heart is the key to finding harmony in the world and working together with others.

With a good heart, we feel emotionally good and emotionally connected. We do not feel emotionally isolated, lonely, depleted, or run down. If we do not have a good heart, there is no richness in our emotional life. In order to have a rich and healthy emotional life, we need a good heart with tenderness and warmth.

When we look at everyone in the world with love and compassion, then our heart is emotionally connected. Our heart is neither frozen nor numb. If we do not have a good heart, if we are without compassion and love, then when we look at the world, it feels foreign and strange. Our heart feels disconnected, or even worse; we may feel hatred, aversion, or prejudice. These are the opposite of a good heart.

If we do not have a good heart, we do not feel anything positive. A good heart is the most important element of our emotional life.

16. True Love

HAVING TRULY UNDERSTOOD and recognized that everyone—our friends, family, neighbors, fellow human beings, and all living beings—are just like we are, we are now much freer to love them. Love can be defined in many ways. True love is the sincere wish for others to have happiness and the conditions necessary for complete and enduring happiness.

We want others to enjoy life, to have a successful journey through each stage of life, to have meaningful work, and to have wonderful relationships. Love means wanting all good things in this world for all others. It arises even with the most mundane of experiences. Something as small as wanting someone to have a good trip is love. Wanting our friends and family to eat healthfully so that they live a long, full life is love. Wanting someone else to have the good experiences we want for ourselves is love. Wanting others to have a good experience when they are meditating, so that they reach enlightenment quickly, is love.

The way to develop a good heart is to aspire to reach the point where this experience of universal love imbues our every thought, action, and attitude. We try to make this a visceral and active inner experience. We make it the experiential filter through which we see everyone. We already have this attitude within us, but it is obscured by our ordinary mind.

Again, this is not just "the right thing to do." We can say instead that it is a practical strategy for both day-to-day happiness and spiritual attainment. It is an essential component of the mind-set to attain enlightenment. Without both Pristine Mind and a good heart, the enlightened state is unreachable.

The kind of love we develop with a good heart is unconditional love. Without the understanding that we are all the same, our love is contingent, it depends on circumstances. For example, when we love someone, typically it is because that person is someone like our girlfriend, boyfriend, or spouse. That kind of love may or may not be conditional. If that person becomes estranged from us and is no longer our lover or spouse, and we no longer love them, then it is conditional love.

But the love of a good heart is universal; it is always unconditional. It is not based on a special relationship. If it is the love for a spouse or partner, and if that love does not change when the relationship ends, then it may be true love. It has to do with recognizing that everyone is just like us and wanting everyone, including the person we are no longer with, to have happiness and the causes of happiness. That is true unconditional love.

True love is always inside us as part of our permanent state. It is not dependent on circumstances. It is not even dependent on circumstances like compatibility, trust, and other factors that can change with time, whether suddenly or gradually. It just is. Whether you are involved in an intimate relationship or not, whether you are together or apart, your love—your sincere desire that the other person be happy, and have all the life circumstances needed to be happy—remains.

If we have this kind of perspective, our love is much deeper, and the experience it causes inside us is profound and very uplifting. We are not focused on that inherently ill-fated quest centered on me, me, me. There are an infinite number of ways to make others happy and to help them have the conditions for happiness. We can give someone good advice, help someone find a job, or provide someone with a good ambience for meditation. This is true love. And as a wonderful side effect, when we make others happy, doing so makes us happy as well.

ROMANTIC LOVE

We all have different notions of what romantic love is. Romantic love is a mental event, often a possessive form of attachment. Ordinary romantic love is not open and relaxed, but narrow and tense. Due to its nature as a form of desire, it can easily lead to anger, jealousy, and rejection. Once we have unconditional love based on a good heart, however, then all forms of love, including romantic love, become more positive and enduring, open and generous. Love becomes less ego-centered. It is rich and inspiring. It provides the lift we need to achieve an enlightened mind.

Romantic love is only truly positive when it is based on a good heart, including the wish for everyone to be happy. A selfless and open-minded perspective on romantic love makes loving relationships more workable and enduring. Without it, "love" is just a form of self-centered desire. Wanting someone as if they were property to possess does not make us a good lover. If we have a good heart, then we are a great lover.

Sometimes relationships and connections deteriorate and end badly. This occurs almost always because one or both partners do not have an attitude of true love that takes precedence over whatever petty annoyances their ordinary minds experience. The relationship may be based on some motive that we mistakenly think is love. Often, it is based on physical or emotional attraction alone. Enduring love is not based on this type of love. If love does not have this enduring characteristic, it is always unhealthy and based on cravings for security in the world of ordinary mind. This is why so many relationships end with great disappointment and suffering.

This does not mean that all relationships should necessarily last forever. What it does mean is that regardless of how long the romance or relationship lasts, and even after it ends, this characteristic of unconditional love remains. On a very practical level, this makes it easier to work out our communications with our partner without needless drama and conflict.

The more we have true love, the better and less complicated our relationships are. We have a larger perspective. The relationship does not deteriorate into a fight for dominance between two egos. We deal with everything that comes up from the perspective of true love. That is the basis of a much more enjoyable, fulfilling, and nurturing relationship. Without this element, love is not genuine.

If our love is a wholehearted caring and interest in other people's happiness and well-being, it is much deeper and makes our relationship more stable. Our relationships then are not just based on fleeting sentiments. There is more sincerity. Because of this, problems do not occur in our relationships very often, and even when difficulties do occur, they are easier to resolve. This deeper understanding of love makes a powerful difference in our connections and interactions.

There are many different misguided interpretations of love. In the extreme examples, people are emotionally, sexually, and physically abused, sometimes even murdered, by those who claim to love them. Terrible crimes happen in the name of "love" every day. Why does romantic love turn bad?

The answer is that such love is not based on the kind of true love we are discussing here. People are unable to experience this selfless attitude as a basis for their love. Romance becomes exclusively egocentric. When the ego does not feel happy and gratified, it becomes enraged at the person it depended on for such good feelings. Of course, other people can never provide the gratification that the ego seeks.

The situation of two people trying to connect with each other can be complicated because their choices and experiences in the relationship are driven by egocentric feelings. Each feels the other person exists only for them and that all aspects of the relationship should be a reflection of their own wants and demands. Their connection is not based on a wish to enjoy the world together. They do not have a wish to really give the other person happiness. It is based on "I want." When such wishes are frustrated, it is easy for the two people to upset each other. Then the relationship deteriorates and, in extreme cases, it can even become dangerous.

It is necessary for both people in a relationship to have a good heart. Then their relationship will be healthier and more fulfilling. Even if they decide not to stay together, having this perspective is helpful to them both. Love does not mean that loved ones never separate, but it does mean that if they stay together, they stay together very harmoniously. Even if they break up, they do so harmoniously. Therefore, any kind of love, especially romantic love, is best when it is based on a good heart.

A Truly Open Mind

In true love our mind and our heart are open to everyone. We are not prejudiced toward any particular individual, culture, or group. We are truly open to all beings. The most sublime experience comes when we sincerely want all beings to be happy. We wish for all beings equally to have happiness and the conditions for happiness.

This does not necessarily mean that we have no conflict with other beings. It just means that having conflict does not signify that we do not love someone. Conflict is created from a disagreement that arises between two people. Genuine love simply transcends that conflict. No matter how much conflict we have with someone, if we still want happiness and the causes of happiness for them, then our love is still unconditional; it goes beyond circumstances.

We may, for example, find conflict or difficulty with one of our parents or siblings. There may even be many times when we do not want to spend much time with them. Yet, still, we want happiness for them. Even if I do not want to spend time with someone, if I want happiness for them, I still love them. I still want happiness and the causes of happiness for them because I have love. It has nothing to do with the conflict. Love is a permanent state that transcends the ups and downs of the relationship. I do not think, "We disagreed; therefore I do not care about her happiness anymore." We may strongly disagree on any number of topics, or we may even be fighting, but still I want the other person to be happy.

If we have an open mind, it means we have a flexible, adaptable mind. We do not get worked up over little things. The more we have the perspective of a good heart, the less reactive we are to situations that some might find provocative. That does not mean we do not get upset at times. We may get upset, but we still have understanding and continue to hold best wishes for that other person. Our love is a permanent state that never leaves us. We have an open-minded perspective that makes it easier for us to forgive and forget. We do not hold grudges.

This is the open-minded, enduring, and universal kind of love that we must cultivate if we are to have intimate connections with loved ones, communicate effectively with others, and attain ultimate enlightenment.

17. Compassion

COMPASSION IS complementary to the quality of love. Just as love is the heartfelt aspiration for others to be happy and to have all the conditions for happiness, compassion is the heartfelt aspiration for others to be free from suffering and from the conditions of suffering.

NOT JUST DURING A CRISIS

Compassion is not just something that we feel for someone who is critically injured, very sick, or in a horrible condition of some kind. People often believe compassion is what we feel when someone has some kind of pain or suffering and we think, "Oh, I feel so sorry for that person." That is one dimension or form of compassion. The compassion that we are describing here is much broader and deeper than that. Like love, it is once again something we can feel for everyone, all the time. It is universal and enduring. Although it may occur in any number of different situations, it does not depend on any particular circumstances.

We can have compassion even for someone who is mentally and physically well, not sick or in crisis. After all, we know that for as long as they live in this world, they will inevitably face physical, mental, and emotional problems on numerous occasions. They will, without any doubt, experience disappointment and sadness, anger and aggression, and a whole array of undesirable circumstances. These things are a part of life. Our compassion makes us wish for them to be free, as much as possible, from these problems and the conditions that contribute to them.

We can have compassion for anyone facing harsh or unwanted circumstances now and in the future, and we can hope that conditions that lead to suffering never accumulate for them. This sincere wish that they do not suffer, that they avoid all physical, mental, and emotional disturbances on every level, is compassion.

What is the basis for this type of compassion? How do we cultivate it?

It is similar to what we talked about with the development of true love. We develop a deep sense of understanding that other people are just like us. We realize, "They want what I want. I want happiness. I do not want suffering. I do not want physical, mental, or emotional pain, discomfort, or unfortunate circumstances. Other beings are the same way. My friends, that stranger over there, and every living being—all are exactly like me. They do not want suffering, just as I do not. I understand that we are exactly the same in this respect. Thus, when they suffer, it is the same as when I suffer."

We comprehend in a deep and meaningful way that others are in the same position we are. We can recognize in an experientially compelling way what they are going through. This makes us sincerely wish for them to be free of everything unwanted, just as we wish that for ourselves. In the same way we do not want to miss our airplane, do not want to be homeless, and do not want our mind to be buffeted about by circumstances like a feather in the wind, other people feel the same way. Their pain is like our pain. We know this and value their experience. And we learn that if we are able to help them, we are going to feel deeply, genuinely good ourselves.

It is relatively easy to be inspired toward this type of compassion when we think of our friends and family, or any community or group with which we identify. We can have the sincere wish for them to be free from all unwanted circumstances and disturbances, be they physical, mental, or emotional. It's easy for most of us to think, "I wish my father didn't have any kind of fear or anxiety. I wish my mother didn't have any kind of doubt or hesitation." Or to think, "I hope that my friends never face any serious illness. I wish that they be free of sickness and problems, and that they be free from anxiety, sadness, anger, aggression, and all negative emotions." But when we understand that everyone is the same in wishing for happiness, and we sincerely wish that nobody should experience suffering, we gain a more expansive perspective, which embraces all living beings.

If we have love and compassion, even if someone starts a conflict with us, we have a better chance of being able to recognize it with compassion, understanding, and tolerance. Instead of reacting impulsively, we might be able to say to ourselves, "Oh, my friend is a little overwhelmed by negative emotions. Negative emotions are controlling his outlook. I know, based on my experiences, that he must be confused or suffering in some way." We recognize that situation, so we will have more patience. Even if the conflict continues and we have a disagreement, we still maintain the perspective that the other person is just like us and only wants to avoid pain. This not only enables us to become more reasonable and compassionate, it also puts us into a generally happier state of mind.

Once we have the perspective that everyone around us wants the very same things that we want, our point of view is more objective, more in line with reality. We are not prejudiced by the interpretations of our own selfishness, fear, and other mental distortions. Compassion serves as a counterbalance to the drives and stresses of our own ego. If we are compassionate, then even when we are furious with someone, we can still want the best for them. Compassionate people are more understanding of the reality that shapes human behavior. They are not distracted by egocentrism and selfishness. So their mental burden is lighter.

Compassion is the wish, not only for our friends and family to be free from physical, mental, and emotional discomfort, but for everyone to be free of these painful states. It applies to people from all walks of life, to the strangers we encounter, to people we will never meet, even to people we may perceive as enemies.

Problems are always caused by selfishness, the constant pursuit of our own happiness while denying, ignoring, or not really understanding the fact that others want happiness just as we do. Problems and disharmony arise from that kind of egocentric attitude. People are abused and treated unfairly by those who lack the understanding that others are just like them. So many problems in this world stem from people denying their fundamental sameness with others.

However, once we understand and truly appreciate in a very deep way this most basic principle of existence, that we all want the same things, then compassion is always within us. It is just a part of us. Anything we do or say comes from that compassion. That is just how we are. We just naturally get along with others because if we have this attitude, conflict does not arise very often.

Guru Rinpoche Padmasambhava says:

The key to helping others effortlessly is to practice boundless compassion.

With this understanding, the experience of compassion is always present as a part of us. This compassionate attitude leads to less conflict, and more harmony and respect, in our lives. Our compassionate actions are contagious; they affect other people, who begin to act in the same way.

SEEING OTHERS' NEEDS

Compassionate people are flexible and do not insist unreasonably on their own way. They see the other side, not just their own—not just what *they* want. Compassion makes us emotionally available and receptive to others' points of view.

Compassionate people do not think the world exists just for them and do not use others for their own benefit. They want success for everyone around them. This creates more success for everyone involved.

Compassion is the foundation for human connection. It is essential to the success of relationships. Compassion is the core of connecting sincerely and harmoniously. Without compassion, we may feel isolation and despair.

We all need to develop our compassion until we experience compassion in every moment and in every interaction of our everyday life. Without compassion, our ego takes over our mind-set and we become preoccupied with ourselves. When compassion is in control, the ego cannot predominate. Compassion is the opposite of ego.

COMPASSION IS COURAGEOUS, STRONG, AND PATIENT

Courage, strength, and patience are linked to compassion because the more we have a sincere wish and desire for others to be free from suffering and pain, the more challenging situations we are willing to face in order to do the things necessary to help others. Nothing will feel too difficult or challenging for us to do in the service of others. Compassion becomes our driving force. Compassion is the measure of our strength of character.

You may have heard of the term *bodhisattva,* used in Buddhist literature. It usually refers to a being of extremely high realization whose sole purpose is to benefit all beings. Bodhisattvas are renowned for having especially great courage or heroism. What defines a bodhisattva's courage? Bodhisattvas are heroic in three different ways: first, they are willingly reborn in this world repeatedly over many eons; second, they resolve to help alleviate the suffering of the infinite number of beings who inhabit the world; and third, they undertake so many difficult challenges for the benefit of beings. A bodhisattva is not afraid of these three things. Why? Because of his or her great compassion. Bodhisattvas act as heroes or role models for us. We can aspire to generate the compassion of a bodhisattva. As our compassionate action increases, we can accomplish amazing things.

It is important to recognize the great power of compassion. When we speak of strong emotions, we may think of an example such as anger, which we all know can even drive a person to violence or murder. But we should see that compassion has just as much strength, except that it is used in the opposite way. Someone who is grounded in compassion has the strength and the courage to do powerful things by fully accessing that compassion.

Patience is also a close companion of compassion. The more love and compassion we have, the more patient we become. The degree to which we have love and compassion is the degree to which we are patient.

Patience does not mean we never get frustrated. Even bodhisattvas, who have devoted their lives to benefiting others, can get upset. Getting upset is not necessarily incompatible with true compassion; in some contexts, it can actually have a very positive effect. The key element in managing impatience and upset is to make sure that we never hold on to such reactions. We must be able to let them go. If we can do that, even impatience and being upset with others can be constructive on some occasions.

Patience also means that we are not afraid of challenges and the time and energy that worthwhile efforts often require. Even when a situation is challenging, if we see a way that our efforts might benefit others, we do not easily give up; we persevere. We may get upset at some point along the way, but we continue to do the job without becoming discouraged. We have more patience for difficult tasks and difficult people. We follow through.

Not giving up on others is a major hallmark of compassion. We are able to maintain some form of connection with others, and we are always working to help them, one way or another. Even if we are disturbed by some aspect of the situation, we try to correct the problem or provide some form of relief to those who suffer from it.

If we have great compassion, we also have a broad mind. A broad mind means we see beyond the immediate circumstances, beyond the present moment in time. We understand the possibilities for change even when they may not be apparent to us in the moment. Because of this, we do not give up on others easily. We stay committed. We see the big picture without fixating on one immediately frustrating aspect of the situation.

LETTING GO IS COMPASSION

In a world of complicated minds swirling with mental events, there are always people who, misguided by the deceptive nature of samsara, seek happiness in ways that create problems for others. We do not have to constantly react to such people. A far more effective way to respond in such a situation is to not get caught up in reacting nor be triggered by the emotions we encounter in others. Even if we do have a reaction, it is important to be able to let it go. We do not need to always react, react, react. There are so many people with complicated minds in this world. To always be reacting to them is exhausting. Most important, it is unnecessary and takes us further and further away from the experience of our Pristine Mind.

If, instead, we understand that this is just the way the world is, full of irrational reactions to mental events that are, in truth, largely irrelevant to what is important, then, even when we do react, we are able to recognize and manage our reaction more appropriately. With this understanding it is much easier to just let our reaction go, giving ourselves more freedom and tolerance, and less agitation and despair. We are much happier when we recognize this than if we are always getting caught up in the disturbed mental events of others. Doing so only makes life very difficult. Avoiding such reactions gives us the deep and ongoing feeling state that is compassion.

The very act of letting go of our reactions in this way is also in itself a form of compassion. It allows the problem to go away. We do not compound the unpleasant nature of the situation. We do not keep repeating it in our mind. We do not hang on to it.

If we are not able to do this, we get stuck in the situation, and it returns to make us suffer the experience again and again. But if we let it go, it is finished. If we need to say something, then we tell the person what we need to express, and then let it go.

It also becomes easier for us to forgive because we know that the other person is just caught up in their own mental events. It is not something personal to us. When someone does something counterproductive, we are able to think, "He's just reacting in his own way. I know he is controlled by his emotions or his ego." The other person simply does not know that they have a choice in how they respond to their mental events. They do not know they have a choice that will let them feel much, much better. We know that, especially with the training of our mind, we can choose not to be caught up in mental events. When we realize that, it is easy to forgive others for their behavior.

Acceptance, forgiveness, and patience are qualities of a good heart. We will not always be patient, but we will have a greater degree of patience and more tolerance of other people's behavior. There is more openness and less struggle. Our mind becomes more suitable for the state of Pristine Mind. The more we have the inner experience of such compassion and unconditional love for others, the easier it is for us to be patient, forgiving, and tolerant. It carries its own reward, so long as it is sincere and genuine.

18. REJOICING

ONCE WE HAVE cultivated a genuine love and compassion for other beings, we don't look at others with envy or jealousy when they are successful and happy. We acknowledge their success and rejoice in their happiness. Celebrating another person's success is the joyous aspect of a good heart.

Once we have this joy, another's triumph does not make us envious or covetous. Instead, we feel genuinely happy for them. It becomes a wonderful experience for us as well as for the other person.

There are many ways others may be doing well. They have just been on a great vacation, they just fell in love with someone wonderful, they just got a promotion, or maybe they just feel great today. With a good heart we are delighted for them. Wanting happiness for others is love, and delighting in the happiness they already have is rejoicing. It is the opposite of envy, a painful and unpleasant emotional state created by ego, the assumption that we can only rejoice in what we ourselves possess, or perhaps possess together with another. In this limiting condition it is only what "I" have that matters and that can contribute to our happiness.

I'm very happy you have a nice girlfriend. I'm very happy you have a nice house. I'm very happy you had a nice vacation. I'm very happy you have a good life. I'm very happy you have a successful career. I'm very happy you are doing very well. I'm very happy your meditation is good. I'm very happy you have developed enlightened qualities. I'm very happy your mind is more pristine. Any happiness or well-being you have, I appreciate it, I rejoice in it, I share in it. This is the aspect of a good heart called rejoicing.

In the absence of this quality, people have a tendency to resist enjoying other people's happiness and success. This form of resistance often creates conflict. The more we feel this resistance, the stronger and more painful it becomes.

Resistance very quickly becomes resentment. First, we resist. The more we revisit the situation, the more we start to experience competitive feelings with that person, and the more it turns into resentment.

The more resentment we build, the more confused and unhappy we are. Not surprisingly, we then begin to behave in ways that only compound our problem.

With resistance and resentment, there is no room for peace and happiness because the world is always providing us with the fodder that feeds our resistance and increases our sense that it's "me against the world."

So without a good heart, there will always be something bothering us. The more we develop a good heart, the less we resist and the more easily we let go. Even if the world around us is chaotic, in the midst of that chaos we can remain in the peace and understanding that our good heart supports and facilitates.

A good heart that rejoices in others' happiness also protects us against developing arrogance when things are going our way. With a good heart we are more natural, more down to earth. We accept that our current good fortune or elevated feeling will not last forever. If we do not have a good heart, when circumstances go well we immediately become proud or boastful, thinking we are better than others. A good heart prevents arrogance.

Good-hearted people usually refrain from doing things that make others angry or jealous. In contrast, arrogant people behave in ways that upset others. They act as if they are superior to other people. Someone with a good heart does not do that. A good heart protects us from many such pitfalls and potential problems within ourselves or with others. A good heart creates happiness and harmony.

Without a good heart, a person often sees the world as hostile, complicated, and unrewarding. But once we have a good heart we have a different perspective. We see and experience the world with more compassion and love. We have understanding, patience, openness, and forgiveness. Even if our surroundings are in a state of chaos, we respond to the circumstances with the inclinations and attitudes of a good heart. That lets us have a harmonious experience no matter where we go and whom we are with.

19. Impartiality

The fourth component of a good heart is impartiality. When our love, compassion, and joy toward others is not subject to any kind of limitation to a particular group, race, or nationality, or to any other class of being, we say it is impartial. The love we develop, the compassion we develop, the sense of rejoicing we develop toward others, is impartial. If it's subject to any kind of restriction, where we think, "Well, I want these people to be happy, but I don't care about that other group," then we are not impartial.

Impartiality means not having any personal bias or prejudice. Our love, our compassion, and our joy are directed at everyone equally, universally, and unconditionally. The quality of impartiality influences all other aspects of a good heart that I have described. For example, an impartial teacher treats his or her students equally, caring about and loving all of them, and wanting each of them to have what they need to grow and flourish. The teacher has the same loving and compassionate feelings and wishes for each of them.

If you have five children in your family, you care for them equally, impartially. You do not treat one badly and another very well. But impartiality goes beyond our own families and groups. With true impartiality, we care not only about humanity but about every life form possessing a mind, no matter how primitive or complex. Where there is such a living being, there are feelings: physically, there is pain and pleasure, and emotionally, there is happiness and sadness. Any such form of living being will have that experience. Therefore it is appropriate to care about everyone equally, love everyone equally, feel compassion toward everyone equally, and rejoice for everyone equally. The greatest good heart extends love and compassion far beyond the boundaries of species.

Limiting one's love to the human species, or to a particular race, nationality, religion, or other human attribute, is not being totally impartial. For example, if I only care about human beings and I don't care about dogs or cats, then my perspective and understanding are inaccurate. Dogs and cats may not be human, but their experience is very similar to our own. They have feelings like we do. Dogs can feel fear. Cats can feel lonely. Because all beings with a mind have mental and emotional pain, desire, and contentment, the most authentic compassion, the most authentic love, and the most authentic joy have no place for any prejudice or bias. The first three boundless attitudes are thus all embraced in the fourth component of a good heart—impartiality.

We can start to apply this principle in a small group, such as a family, a circle of friends, or a team of co-workers. We must regularly make a conscious effort to treat all the members of that group equally, feel love toward them equally, feel compassion toward them equally, and rejoice for all of them equally. This is not just an exercise you do by yourself; you need to remind yourself to do it in the context of your daily life. Then, expand the group to include the larger community. Ultimately, this must expand to all living beings from all groups and species.

This creates a harmonious experience. What we mean by a good heart here is not simplistic. Sometimes people say things to each other like, "You are so good-hearted. You did something so nice today." In this way, we may use the term "good-hearted" to mean something very simple, to describe a relatively nice person. But in the sense in which we use the term here, there are many levels, degrees, and dimensions of a good heart. Once we understand that everyone is just like us, it gives us a more accurate perspective. Our perception, then, transcends superficial boundaries. A truly good heart has no boundaries at all: our compassion, love, and joy extend to every living being that feels; and our good heart is open to every being with physical and mental sensations. This has nothing to do with their characteristics, whether they are close to us, or even whether they are human. Instead, it has to do with the fact that they have feelings, emotions, sensations, and mind. Any being that has sensations, emotions, feelings, pain and pleasure, is an object for our caring attitude and action.

The reality is that everyone wants happiness and does not want suffering. Everyone wants these equally, so it only makes sense to honor their wishes equally, and to do what we can to help others achieve those wishes.

20. The Benefits of a Good Heart

There are so many levels, degrees, and dimensions of a good heart. If we think of it as something simple, it is easy to overlook its importance. It is crucial that we let ourselves experience the very different way our whole being feels when our good heart is strong and fervent, and at the front and center of our experience of life.

If we possess the four components of a good heart, our emotions are more positive and warm. All our thoughts, beliefs, and habits are colored by these four positive mental attitudes. As a result, our feelings, emotions, and experiences are gentler, less negative, and less confusing. All our physical actions, our speech, and our other mental activities are colored by these positive emotions, these four positive attitudes. When we are in that mental state, what we say and how we act come from a good heart. Our experience of the world becomes more majestic and open. It is vibrant, radiant, and sublime.

Our state of mind is no longer harsh and austere, like the winter, with its cold winds, gusts of snow, and sheets of ice that so dominate the landscape of our mind. Instead, it is like spring, with the temperature soothing and warm, flowers in bloom, and gentle breezes blowing. Our heart is no longer frigid. The weather in our mind is beautiful when we have a good heart.

Even when negative emotions appear from time to time, as they will, they exert less control over us. When bad habits and negative emotions have too much control, there is frequent conflict and resentment. In contrast, when we develop a good heart, then most relationship problems, misunderstandings, and arguments vanish naturally.

If we have a good heart, conflict can be easily resolved. But without love and compassion, arguing and fighting can sometimes take on the character of not just a disagreement but an all-out war. We do not care about the other person or the other side; we only want to defeat them. When two people want to defeat each other, even small problems become larger problems and conflicts escalate. If we have a good heart, however, even big problems become smaller and conflicts dissolve.

THE SOURCE OF ALL POSITIVE QUALITIES

Even when we have a good heart, of course, negative emotions like anger can appear and temporarily obscure our good heart. At those times we need to recognize that we have become caught up in mental events and negative emotions. When those events settle down and pass by, we can return to our usual good-hearted state. Most of the time, however, once we have developed this good heart, we think, talk, and act in accordance with our good heart. It is simply a part of who we are. When we talk to someone, our attitude displays that good heart. And from that display, good things naturally flow.

Even if we scold someone about their mistakes or inappropriate actions, we approach it from our good heart. If criticism comes from compassion and love, then it is positive and the other person is more likely to experience our concern even if they do not like the criticism. But if the criticism comes from jealousy or other negative emotions, then it is negative. An action alone is often not as important as the attitude behind the action.

Sometimes people think that if we have compassion it means we are always peaceful and smiling, maybe even deferential, but that is not necessarily true. With compassion we are free to speak more directly and straightforwardly, because we can trust in the goodness from which we speak. The other person will often sense that and feel loved rather than chastised. We can confront someone without aggression.

This is important because sometimes the greatest compassion requires directness. If we want to help someone we care about, we may even need to speak sharply and forcefully at times. With a good heart, our frustration does not come from our ego; it comes from our compassion. Compassion, then, may come in different forms. It may be very peaceful and gentle in its origin and yet appear very angry. It all depends on the nature of the heart from which it springs.

For example, if your child knows that your underlying attitude and the source of your actions is love and compassion, then the child will accept your anger and discipline. If the child does not know that your attitude is fundamentally positive, then your anger will deeply hurt the child's feelings. Children need to be educated that a caring parent's love can come in many forms. They need to understand it's the underlying attitude that's important. Once they know that love does not come just from giving them presents, then even if the parents act impatiently or angrily in a particular situation, such as losing their temper, the child will know that the parent's actions come from the genuine love and compassion of a good heart, and their feelings will not be badly hurt. There are so many "methods" foisted on parents for raising children that go in and out of style. If parents make sure their actions arise from true love and compassion, not selfishness, then the particular method matters so much less. But you can't assume you have love and compassion just because you are dealing with your child. You need to consciously and deliberately develop your attitude of love and compassion.

The same is true with couples. If the relationship is based on both people having a good heart, then conflicts and arguments will not threaten the relationship. The relationship will remain based on mutual trust. For example, if the partners know that it's more than just gifts and special events that are the expressions of each one's love for the other, then they will take the long view and not just consider the short term. They will both always want each other to be happy and to have the conditions for happiness, and they will both always want each other not to suffer or have any conditions of suffering. If one of them is selfish, however, conflicts can destroy the relationship. If this mutual, reciprocal love is not present, then even doing good things for each other will not help—it's actually deceptive, because the underlying attitude of love is not there. You can't assume you automatically have love and compassion for each other just because you are a couple. You both need to consciously and deliberately develop your attitude of love and compassion for each other.

All positive emotions are recharged and operate smoothly through a good heart. If we have a good heart, then our other positive emotions become stronger and more stable. A good heart makes us a good person. It causes us to treat others kindly and to forgive easily. It causes us to behave ethically, patiently, sincerely, and in a trustworthy manner at all times.

If we lack this good heart, then we are never really living completely, and we are missing this most beautiful experience of being in the world.

Some degree of a good heart is essential if we want to live or die with contentment. It is the true source of all positive feelings we can have in life. And it is also an essential element of the experience of Pristine Mind. Without a good heart, access to Pristine Mind is blocked by the constrictions of the ego. A good heart is essential to having an open path to our Pristine Mind.

A Good Heart and Marriage

Our current culture takes a materialistic view of almost everything, including romantic love and spirituality. This attitude creates a great imbalance in our lives. For example, when couples plan their wedding, so much attention is paid to external conditions—the perfect bridal gown, the expensive rings, the fragrant flowers, the delicious food, the lavish party—that their inner experience of the event is often devoid of the beauty of a good heart. All the attention on material things can cause them to miss the elements that are most important to a marriage: a sincere motivation and a good heart. Without these, the ceremony becomes devoid of meaning.

In marriage, having a good heart means we are in a genuine and deep state of love that asks, "How can I bring happiness and fulfillment to my partner's life? How can I prevent my spouse from suffering?" That principle is critically important to all marriages because it focuses each partner on the other's experience instead of fixing attention on their own benefit and pleasure.

If the couple does not have this internal state of genuine love as the central experience of the relationship, then the wedding is exclusively materialistic. It has no heart. A dress is just a bundle of fabric worn once, and the bouquet will last only hours before wilting. After the wedding, when the dancing stops, the cake is eaten, and everyone returns home, then without the true love of a good heart, the bride and groom might feel disappointingly strange and empty. If we pay too much attention to material items that we pursue with our ordinary minds, then we miss the importance of having a good heart.

Before people get married, or even before they begin a relationship, they should develop a good heart through cultivating the four boundless attitudes of love, compassion, joy, and impartiality. A good heart, with which we are genuinely wishing for the happiness of the other person, is essential to the success of any marriage.

THE STUDENT-TEACHER CONNECTION

Whenever you have connections with friends, family, or groups, the most essential part of the connection is a good heart and sincerity. The same is true for connections with teachers, particularly spiritual teachers. The student must receive the teachings with enthusiasm and true respect for the teacher and the teachings. Then the student is qualified to receive the teachings.

Having a teacher isn't about selfishly receiving the teacher's energy. Many people say, "Oh, I went to see this spiritual teacher who had this great presence, a nice energy." They may enjoy that energy for many years, hanging around with that teacher, but they are not really interested in receiving teachings. There are many people who do this. Instead of receiving and contemplating teachings, they just spend time enjoying the energy of the teacher, allowing the teacher's energy to recharge what they think is their spiritual experience. But that is not the best way to be a student. There is a Tibetan saying: "The worst student is like a rock sitting at the bottom of the sea. The best student is like a cup filled with pure water." No matter how long a rock has been sitting in the sea, if you take it out of the water and put it on the shore, after a few moments it dries out because it has not absorbed any of the water. On the other hand, a cup can not only hold the water poured into it, the water can even be used to slake others' thirst.

If you are just seeking the energy and presence of a teacher instead of taking the teachings to heart, then once your teacher passes away, or is not around, you are left with nothing, because the teachings have not penetrated your mind. But when your mind holds the teacher's wisdom, then you can benefit yourself, and your good heart will naturally pour over to others. Then, even when the teacher is no longer there, you can maintain the lineage of the teachings through your own dedication and wisdom. You are not dry and empty of wisdom or compassion like that stone on the shore.

When you spend time with a teacher, the teacher's energy and presence are not what is most important. What is most valuable is receiving the teacher's authentic lineage, wisdom, and instructions, like receiving the water poured into your cup, and following those instructions by mastering your meditation practice and developing your good heart. That's what all authentic lineage holders have done. When Guru Rinpoche Padmasambhava came to Tibet, he assembled twenty-five main disciples. When the disciples spent time with him, of course they appreciated his presence and energy, but most important, they absorbed his wisdom teachings, spread these teachings throughout Tibet, and preserved the teachings for future generations. Likewise, the Buddha's disciples enjoyed the Buddha's presence and they enjoyed the Buddha's energy, but what they appreciated most, and what was most important to them, was the Buddha's wisdom teachings.

Also, absorbing and practicing the teachings are the best form of appreciation for the teacher, and also cause the most happiness for the teacher.

Padmasambhava says:

> If you want a spiritual master who holds you in his heart,
> You must live and practice according to the master's teachings
> and advice.

A good heart is not only something for the student to develop; it is also essential for the teacher. The teacher should be one who does not just repeat book knowledge, but who has a strong background of receiving teachings from authentic masters, and who lives by the principles of realization, meditation, and a good heart. Having such a qualified teacher is necessary in order for the student to benefit and, ultimately, to attain true enlightenment.

Guru Rinpoche Padmasambhava says:

> If you want to perceive the nature of reality, then you need
> a qualified spiritual master.

The great master Patrul Rinpoche called the highest form of good heart, known as *bodhichitta,* the most important quality of a spiritual teacher. Bodhichitta is not just an ordinary good heart; it is the ultimate expression of a good heart. Patrul Rinpoche said that without bodhichitta, a teacher could be dangerous. Why dangerous? Because as students build trust in a teacher, the more powerful that teacher becomes and the greater his or her influence over the students; if the teacher does not have bodhichitta, the students can be misled or manipulated. But a teacher who has bodhichitta will never lead a student in the wrong direction.

When both of these conditions are met—the qualified teacher and the qualified student—then the Pristine Mind experience, unconditional happiness, and ultimate enlightenment can manifest.

EDUCATION AND A GOOD HEART

Most of us are inclined toward a good heart. But we need to develop this tendency, nurture it, and bring it to the forefront of our awareness. We do that, in part, through educating ourselves about the qualities of love and compassion. If we are not educated in this area, and we do not explore or pay attention to nurturing a good heart, we will not develop it. Instead, our negative, egocentric thoughts and emotions will dominate our mind. In that negative environment, positive tendencies and experiences don't grow. We will not fully experience the positive thoughts and feelings that, along with our Pristine Mind, lead us to enlightenment.

People who have a good heart develop these qualities by first learning to value the qualities of love and compassion, and then dedicating themselves to cultivating love and compassion in practice and experience.

A good heart makes life meaningful and rich. We feel we are living fully, because our heart is warm and full. Today, especially, there is a need for parents and educators to teach young people how to develop these traits. We need to be explicit in teaching people of all ages the benefits of compassion, love, joy, and impartiality. It must become our priority if we are to have a happy society.

Why do people experience so much anger, jealousy, and resentment? Partly because we are surrounded by so many influences that encourage us to express ourselves in a negative way. We are exposed to so many models of resentment and anger. Children are taught resentment very early on. They are urged to express, "You hurt my feelings." But they don't often say, "I want my brothers and sisters to be happy." How many children are saying that? More often we hear them say, "I need this game. I want more toys." Children generally are taught more about resentment and entitlement than they are about love and compassion. They don't hear about love and compassion very much at all. We simply cannot take the development of a good heart for granted. Like any other life skill, it must be taught. Teaching children explicitly how to have a good heart when they are young will help reduce bullying and mistreatment as they grow up.

We can still have a good heart even if we feel anger. However, the more we pay attention to such tendencies as anger, the more powerful they become. Just as anger becomes more powerful when we feed it with our attention, compassion is rendered less powerful because we have not shown it enough attention.

We need to create the right circumstances to develop the love and compassion necessary for a good heart. Spending time with people who themselves have love and compassion and being influenced by them helps generate love and compassion in us. Listening to talks and reading books by people who have real compassion, as well as meditating, are all helpful conditions and create the environment for developing a good heart.

Living Fully

The quality of your life depends on your state of mind. If you have a good state of mind, you will definitely have a good life, a good death, and a good experience after this life. Everyone wants to have a good life, but all too often people do not know how to find it. People try all sorts of different ways. Some become famous, but they find that even fame does not work. Many famous people are very, very unhappy. Some people become materially wealthy, but even if they are affluent, wealth cannot bring them happiness if they are internally poor.

With the most perfect state of mind, we can experience the highest form of a good life. Our joy is limitless and enduring. That perfect state of mind is the combination of Pristine Mind and a good heart. They go together.

When we are in connection with that state of mind, our joy permeates our life on physical, mental, and emotional levels. We have a sense of comfort and well-being all the time, in each and every moment. As our compassion and love flourish and grow, we feel completely connected because we are not rejecting or disconnecting from the world around us into an inner world of ego based self-absorption. By virtue of that genuine connection to the world, we are free from loneliness.

Once our mind enters this perfect state, we experience a happiness that is not just a momentary good mood, where one moment we are elated and the next moment upset. Mentally and emotionally we have a deep sense of comfort. Everything in our life is imbued with a grounded yet majestic sense of contentment and well-being. Once our mind is in a really perfect state, even our material things, our status and other external conditions, contribute to our happiness and fulfillment.

The three principles we have now discussed—realization, meditation, and a good heart—are necessary for us to live in this world fully and authentically. They are essential for our life to be complete and integrated. They become especially necessary at the moment of death and beyond. When these three principles become the driving force of our life and its mental and emotional experiences, we quickly develop a very deep confidence in the importance they have to our happiness and fulfillment.

Without these three principles, our mind is chaotic, homeless, and buffeted about by habits, belief systems, and ordinary thoughts. Ordinary thoughts carry us from place to place, and there's no telling where we will end up. Our minds will almost always be lost in these mental events. We do not know what our destination will be, since it depends on our circumstances.

Once we have a good heart, realization, and meditation, we have more unconditional happiness. We are more capable of success in this world, and we are also able to be content and comfortable under any circumstances. If you live by these three principles, your life has real integrity and authenticity. This is why developing a good heart is so important. Once you have developed your good heart, then your realization, your meditation, your happiness, and your worldly and spiritual success all flourish.

Padmasambhava says:

> The joy of meditation is realization that is free from mental
> events, distractions, and dullness of mind.
> The joy of compassion is impartiality free from bias
> or prejudice.

The joy of experience is one's own Pristine Mind, free from
distortions.
The joy of generosity is freedom from the grasp of attachment
and expectation.
The joy of wealth is to realize that all possessions are illusions.
If you know your own true nature, there's no restlessness.
This is effortless joy.

PART FIVE

Enlightenment: Fully Awakened Pristine Mind

You can search throughout time and space and you will not
find enlightenment.
Enlightenment is the innermost nature of mind.
Do not seek enlightenment anywhere else.

—*Essence of Secrets Tantra*

21. What Is Enlightenment?

M ANY PEOPLE BELIEVE that enlightenment is mystical, that it just happens mysteriously without any logic behind it. Some people think it is an unattainable state, reserved only for someone with the rarest qualities. Others think enlightenment is simply an exceptionally good mood or a state in which our mind has no thoughts. Some believe it is a special, sudden experience that overtakes us, some kind of altered state, like the sudden change that one might feel from taking mind-altering drugs. Indeed, there are so many different ideas about enlightenment that it is very important that we understand just what enlightenment really is.

The Conditions for Enlightenment

Without the necessary conditions, enlightenment cannot happen any more than flowers can grow in a hostile environment. The right conditions for flowers are not present in a dark, frozen cave. Many elements are needed for a flower to grow, such as soil, light, water, and the right temperature. Everything in our world arises only under the right conditions and the required environment.

In the same way, when we talk about attaining enlightenment, we are talking about the right conditions and environment for enlightenment to blossom and grow.

What conditions are needed for enlightenment? We need to have the right state of mind: open, compassionate, positive, and beautiful. Primarily, we need the three principles: realization, meditation, and a good heart. These conditions generate a different and extraordinary environment in our mind, an environment that supports enlightenment. Guru Rinpoche Padmasambhava says:

If you cultivate positive attitudes and circumstances,
It helps your mind to naturally go in the right direction.
If your mind goes in the right direction,
It helps to improve and increase your meditation experience.
If you develop the right meditation experience,
It helps you to quickly attain perfect enlightenment.

Although we often say that we "attain" or "achieve" enlightenment, it is not actually something that occurs off in the distance or sometime in the distant future. If our mind is pristine, nirvana is here, right now, in this very moment. If our mind is polluted, samsara is here, right now, in this moment. Everything happens in this moment.

Our state of mind determines our reality, right now, in this moment. Therefore, the most important thing is to have the right mind-set right now in this moment. The only thing standing between us and enlightenment right now is our mental events. That's it. When our mental events are no longer present, enlightenment becomes naturally evident, whether we seek it or not. Enlightenment is essentially the complete, permanent absence of distorted mind, thus letting us experience the deep and abiding inner state that lies beneath mental events. Our mind becomes completely pristine without any negative thoughts or emotions that cause suffering. Our mind becomes completely healthy and perfect. This is the true meaning of enlightenment.

The Four Stages of Awakening

In the previous parts of this book, we discussed realization and meditation—how to realize Pristine Mind and how to meditate in Pristine Mind. We explained the techniques necessary to realize that the mind is pristine, what that experience or realization feels like, and then how to practice meditation based on that experience. We studied what factors are most important, and what methods we should use. We also explained the critical role played by cultivating a good heart.

If we realize and abide in Pristine Mind, we are doing meditation. Once we are able to do that for longer and longer periods of time and are able to maintain and expand our good heart, then our experience transforms, and certain changes take place in our mind.

Those changes are the process of awakening our enlightened nature. In fact, transformation, liberation, and awakening all occur from remaining in Pristine Mind. With that foundation established, it is time to explain the enlightenment that occurs based on this practice.

The clearest, most direct presentation of enlightenment that I know is Dzogchen master Mipham Rinpoche's description in his extraordinary Dzogchen text *The Spacious Path of Bliss*. In this text, Mipham Rinpoche demystifies enlightenment and the path to enlightenment. His explanation comes from personal experience, and he presents it in a very straightforward way. It is not written academically or based on intellectual understanding. It is universal and timeless, so everyone can know it and benefit from it. It makes the understanding of enlightenment accessible to all of us.

Various texts talk about the stages of enlightenment, but many of them are obscure and difficult to understand. In contrast, *The Spacious Path of Bliss* is direct, experiential, and yet profound. I will describe it to you as I understand it. What follows now is based on this great teaching of Mipham Rinpoche.

There are four different stages that occur when we awaken to our Pristine Mind. These make up the path to enlightenment. Whether or not someone is enlightened has to do with whether or not they have progressed through these four stages. In describing them, Mipham Rinpoche clarifies elements of enlightenment that often confuse people into thinking enlightenment is mysterious or mystical.

Sometimes people may find it difficult to understand enlightenment because they have no reference point for what enlightenment truly is. Understanding these four stages helps us to clarify where we are on our path of enlightenment. If someone claims to have an education, we can verify their credentials at the college or university that they attended. If they claim to be a lawyer, we can confirm whether that is true by checking their records at the state bar association. While enlightenment has no certification board, the validity of a person's level of enlightenment is apparent based on the signs of these four stages that manifest, as I will describe below. It is not mysterious. It is definable and describable.

Among other signs of progress in attaining enlightenment, two key changes, or "awakenings," occur in becoming enlightened. First, negative tendencies, thoughts, and emotions lose strength. Second, the experience of Pristine Mind grows, and there is greater access to it. If these two things are happening, then enlightenment is happening.

The more clouds dissipate, the more we see the blue sky beyond them. In the same way, the more our ordinary thoughts and emotions fade away, the more we can access Pristine Mind. The more our mental events dissolve, the more our Pristine Mind awakens. Gradually, thoughts, emotions, and other mental events can no longer control us. We have complete freedom to access the wonderful experience of our Pristine Mind. If that capacity is unfolding within us, then enlightenment is emerging from within us. If these two things are not happening inside us, then enlightenment is not occurring.

Although we may talk about a path to attaining enlightenment, actually enlightenment is not just a single end point, but a process of growth. There is a gradual awakening of our enlightened nature. Completely perfect enlightenment is merely the end result of that process of gradual improvement.

We will now turn to the four stages of enlightenment described by Mipham Rinpoche.

22. The First Stage of Awakening

The first stage of awakening described by Mipham Rinpoche is the experience of someone who has just begun to practice Pristine Mind meditation. In this stage, the beginner has recognized their Pristine Mind and is just starting to have momentary experiences of resting in their fundamental nature. They are beginning to have some experiences of awakening. In many ways, however, they are still just like an ordinary person caught in the limitations of the ordinary mind seeking happiness in the world of samsara.

As a beginning practitioner, we may glimpse the true nature of our Pristine Mind in a moment of realization. We may even be able to rest in Pristine Mind for a few minutes during meditation. But, as a beginner, our mind is still chaotic and largely uncontrollable. At this first stage of awakening, even though we may have recognized our Pristine Mind and can access it from time to time, our mind is still mostly lost and aimlessly drifting all over the place, like a feather in the wind.

Mipham Rinpoche says that at this first stage, our concepts, thoughts, emotions, and other mental events seem to be harmful obstacles to our experience of Pristine Mind. Our thoughts are judgmental; our moods vary from elation to melancholy. Many thoughts make us uncomfortable, self-conscious, or angry, while other thoughts make us anxious, worried, or sad. There is an almost constant turbulence in our mind. That is why we say our thoughts arise as harmful obstacles, even if some of our thoughts appear positive. When we are a beginning meditation practitioner, our experience is mostly just like anyone else's experience. We may have had a little bit of an experience of Pristine Mind, but we have not yet experienced the big change that occurs when we are further along in our connection to our Pristine Mind.

Mipham Rinpoche says at this first stage, our mental events are like waves on the surface of the ocean, with thoughts arising continuously, and it's difficult to calm them down. Mipham Rinpoche says there are so many emotions, habits, and tendencies. Also, he says our mind is like a piece of paper blown about by the wind, buffeted by circumstances. This is what it is like for most people in ordinary mind. People have hopes and fears accompanied by many different forms of mental and emotional discomfort. In such a state, no matter who we are, when all these thoughts and emotions are rampantly out of control, a beginner suffers just as other people suffer.

At this stage along the path to enlightenment, when habits, thoughts, and emotions arise, Mipham Rinpoche says, we have difficulty recognizing that these things are just mental events. It is hard to remember that they are just our own projections and our own perceptions.

When we are a beginning meditator, our mental events are still very hard to tolerate. Just because we begin meditating today does not mean that tomorrow our mind will be comfortable. It takes time to change. If we practice diligently, changes can occur quickly, but in the beginning, we will all struggle. This is normal and not something that should discourage us.

When we first start to meditate, we still have the same hopes and fears and anxieties that we did before we started. Mipham Rinpoche says that especially at this time we need to be patient and continue to remain in Pristine Mind. Do not follow mental events, be aware of whether or not mental events are taking over our awareness, and be mindful. If mental events have clouded our mind, we need to recognize that and remind ourselves that they are just events, and return to abiding in Pristine Mind as best we can. Our frustration at this time is normal. It by no means implies that we are failing at meditation or cannot make progress.

When a student asks their teacher, "What do I do when my mind wanders?" the answer is that no matter what occurs, simply recognize this and return to awareness; remain in Pristine Mind as best as you are able. When our mind wanders or any sounds or sensations occur, we should try not to identify with that mental event, not follow it, and not get caught up in it. We just try to remain in Pristine Mind; then everything else takes care of itself. We remain present and try to be aware of our awareness and nothing else. There is nothing more we need to do.

Mipham Rinpoche says, "Don't get upset if many thoughts arise." W should not become discouraged or feel like our meditation is not working. We are simply not yet at a stage where we are free from thoughts arising. We are not yet able to see the effects of meditation working. It is working, however, even though we may not feel like it is.

The best course of action is to be patient, continue to remain present, get more familiar with our pristine awareness itself, and persevere. We are not wasting our time. We are giving our mind time to settle.

Losing patience after first starting to meditate would be like going for walks for a day or two and then thinking, "Oh I still haven't changed. I can't run a marathon yet. My health will never improve. Exercise isn't working." We need to learn the proper techniques and take the time to build endurance if we are going to see results. When we begin meditating, it is similar.

At first it can be challenging to maintain our meditation for even ten or fifteen minutes. It feels as if time passes so slowly because when we first start meditating, our mind is very active. It is the ongoing mental activity, our mental events, that makes our meditation feel like a struggle at first. But at that time especially, we need to have great patience. We need to continue practicing meditation and not give up or lose hope, but be patient. Mipham Rinpoche stresses that at this stage patience is the key to progressing on the path to enlightenment.

23. The Second Stage of Awakening

As we become more practiced in abiding in Pristine Mind for longer periods of time, gradually our mental environment changes. Unlike the first stage, where mental events have full control, the second stage is marked by thoughts and emotions losing their strength to a noticeable extent.

This does not mean mental events do not still arise. They do. But a substantial reduction occurs in the disruption they cause in our meditation experience, because the three aspects of our realization are deepening, becoming more pronounced, and we are remaining in Pristine Mind for longer periods of time. The power of our meditation and realization fuels our awakening because our mind is pristine to a greater degree in almost every moment. While our mind may not often be completely pristine, it is no longer totally obscured as it was when we began our practice. Our mind is covered by a mere haziness, with fewer formed thoughts and mental events. Our thoughts and emotions no longer have much strength or control over us because they no longer get all our attention.

When we were at the first stage of awakening, we may have experienced Pristine Mind from time to time, but most of our attention was on mental events; therefore the mental events were stronger and more powerful.

In the second stage of awakening, mental events get less of our attention, because we are more immersed in our Pristine Mind. As a result, thoughts, emotions, and tendencies are not always present in our mind; they lose the prominence they had in our mind. While this is bad news for our ego-based mental events, it is good news for us as meditation practitioners. It is the critical sign of the second stage—the loss of strength of thoughts, emotions, and other mental events.

This is also the first true sign of awakening. If we want to know whether our meditation practice is going well, we should look for this sign: How powerful are our mental events? If they still have the same power, especially if we have been meditating for many years, it means our meditation is not working and we should consult with a qualified teacher. But if they have less power, if we have more control over our mental events, it means our meditation practice and our mind are improving.

Mipham Rinpoche says that at this second stage, thoughts, emotions, and other mental events will continue to arise and buzz around our mind, but they are much more bearable. They are not as harsh or as hard to bear as they were at the first stage of awakening. Even though the waves of thoughts and emotions continue to rise and fall from time to time, we are more able to be tolerant with the knowledge that they will pass and we are not overwhelmed by the experience. If we can imagine the way a horse barely pays attention to a fly, casually chasing it away with a wave of its tail, in the same way, thoughts may buzz past our consciousness from time to time, but they do not cause a strong and disruptive reaction. We notice them but stay attuned to our awareness, or at least quickly return to it.

As we remain in Pristine Mind for longer periods of time, our state of mind shifts. Mipham Rinpoche compares it to a spring breeze. In the winter, the harsh, cold wind wields sharp gusts that cut to the bone and are hard to bear. But when spring comes, the environment and temperature change, so the wind does not wield those disrupting weapons any longer. Instead, the spring wind is a gentle, light breeze.

Similarly, through our practice of Pristine Mind meditation, our mental environment becomes warmer and softer. There is a noticeable shift in our perception. Any mental events we experience are comparatively smooth and create less turbulence. When mental events arise, we are aware of how they function, and we know about their fleeting and ephemeral nature. We know that if we dismiss them without paying them much attention, they cannot be as turbulent as they once were before we understood them. They feel softer and gentler.

Encouraged by seeing this change in our experience, we will feel more enthusiasm for our meditation practice and more delight in our actual meditation itself. We begin to gain confidence in our meditation.

As Mipham Rinpoche says, gaining this enthusiasm and confidence in our practice is the greatest gift one can receive. This is an experience one cannot buy at any price. This is the precious gift that arises at this second stage on our journey to enlightenment.

TRANSFORMATION AND LIBERATION

Three transformations must occur through our meditation practice for us to become enlightened: our experience of Pristine Mind must manifest and deepen; the strength of our distorted mental events must dissipate; and our good heart must expand.

These go hand in hand with one another. These transformations cause a profound shift in the mode of our perception as they evolve. Under these circumstances, and only under these circumstances, enlightenment can happen.

These transformations make themselves known in the following way. As our thoughts and emotions change from negative to positive, the contents of our mind change; splendor, clarity, beauty, and love slowly replace the agitation and fear of the world we once created with our mental events. As the contents of our mind shift, the way we perceive shifts. Instead of seeing things through our ordinary mind's distorted filter of habits, beliefs, and negative emotions, we see things more accurately and clearly.

And the more our perception shifts, the more the contents of our mind shift. This is a positive feedback loop between our perception and the contents of our mind that leads to continuous improvement. They feed each other as part of our process of change. Prior to our commitment to meditating, this reciprocal process worked in the opposite direction; when we perceived things negatively through the filters of fear and the futile desires of ordinary mind, then the contents of our mind became more negative. As the contents of our mind became negative, we perceived our world more negatively. Now we are reversing that process. It is really that simple.

The more we perceive our true nature, the more all these troubling experiences we had, which still dominated our life as a beginning meditation practitioner, slowly but noticeably begin to dissipate. All habits and negative emotions dissolve because they cannot exist independently of our attention. They arise from our misperception of their importance. So now that we see accurately, they all fade away and dissipate.

The shift in our mental environment changes the tone of mental events.

They no longer have the power to make us suffer or make us confused. They are no longer able to affect us. This creates a real and significant improvement in our mental and emotional experience: our mind becomes more healthy and natural. Such a shift in perception slowly continues, and complete enlightenment comes yet closer.

KNOWING OUR INTERNAL WEATHER

The primary and most noticeable difference that we will see between the first stage and the second stage is that our distorted mental events begin to lose their strength. The other significant difference is that in the second stage, we become an expert in our understanding of how mental events arise and disappear. We truly understand how mental events operate, work, and function.

Meteorologists are experts at understanding weather patterns. A meteorologist understands air pressure, temperature, and cloud formation, and how certain conditions create certain weather. In the same way, as we meditate more and more, we become more and more familiar with the "weather patterns" of our mind. We know what conditions lead to what types of internal weather. We become an expert in how various experiences arise and disappear. With that understanding of the internal patterns of mental events, we gradually reduce their disruptive effect on our reconnection with the pristine state of mind. This makes a tremendous difference in our experience of the world.

We learn that if we disregard our Pristine Mind and follow our mental event, the mental event gains more power over us. Once we become absorbed in it, the more we take it seriously, the more power it gains. But now that we notice that fact and understand how our mental events operate, we can liberate ourselves from the power those events have over us. So whether our mental events are positive or negative, they don't affect us as much because we know how they appear and disappear.

If we practice meditation, mental events simply cannot operate during that window of time in which we are meditating. If we meditate for twenty to forty minutes every day, there is a regular break in our mental events. They are losing their territory and their control over us. They may regain control from time to time, but they are not in full control anymore. The more we abide in Pristine Mind, the more we realize mental events are like an illusory army that we increasingly are able to vanquish, merely by paying less attention to them.

It is important to emphasize that at this second stage of awakening, it is not that we just *think* of mental events as illusions, but we actually *experience* increasingly that all mental events are illusory. They are like the pesky fly buzzing around the horse, which pays little attention to it. The mental events are noticed, but they hardly disrupt our more natural state of mind.

This is the way enlightenment occurs—gradually. Everything we see, think, and hear shifts more and more with time.

At the second stage, we, as the practitioner, feel more mentally, emotionally, and spiritually powerful because our mental events have softened. We feel a greater sense of well-being. Our happiness is more stable because mental events can no longer undermine, disturb, or rob us of our happiness or dictate our experience. All of these things occur naturally when our mental and emotional experiences, our mental events, lose their control.

24. THE THIRD STAGE OF AWAKENING

IN ORDINARY MIND, both positive and negative thoughts have a big impact on us. But at the third stage of awakening, mental events have hardly any impact, either positive or negative. Our happiness is no longer dependent on mental events, no longer dependent on outside conditions or circumstances. Our mental environment is completely different at this stage.

BECOMING FRIENDS WITH OUR MENTAL EVENTS

In the third stage of awakening, Mipham Rinpoche says that mental events transform from being enemies to being harmless, even friendly. Everything in our being feels very smooth, and our thoughts and emotions are mainly positive. Mental events are less influential in all ways, not just the harmful ways, than they were in the first or second stages of enlightenment; they simply lose their importance.

Unlike when we began our practice, thoughts that arise in the third stage of awakening are no longer harmful. Negative mental events have disappeared, and the remaining events tend to be positive and joyful, like helpful friends, improving our internal experience of life. In an ordinary state of mind, including the first stage of awakening, negative thoughts and emotions support and empower one another. Those negative thoughts, emotions, and habits are working together. Our mental projections and perceptions feed and strengthen each other. In the third stage, our perceptions and our mental environment are different, and remarkably positive. This makes it difficult for negative or harmful thoughts to form.

In the middle of a hot summer day in New York City, it is impossible for ice to form across a lake in Central Park. The ice cannot form because the environment does not support it. In the same way, for someone at this third stage of awakening, it is difficult for any harmful thoughts or negative emotions to form. The mental environment does not support negative mental events; therefore, any mental or emotional experiences that arise are harmless and not of great consequence. The mind, under most circumstances, is in an almost completely pristine state.

Whatever mental events do arise have very little influence. At this stage, they neither help us nor harm us because the mental environment is more and more pure. Even positive mental events do not provide help as they may have done in our ordinary mind. They are like candles burning in sunlight; they make no difference. Without their influence, we are free to have a relaxed, fluid, and powerful mind.

How does the third stage of awakening occur? The more we develop our experience of the three realizations, the more we widen the gap between mental events; the more we experience Pristine Mind, the more mental events dissolve, and the more positive are those that remain. Negative thoughts no longer arise, because they cannot function in an environment that does not support them. In order to resume having those reactions to our mental events that we once had, we would need to revert to our ordinary mind. But in this third stage, our mind-set is very beautiful, and whatever remaining mental events arise in it, we can for the most part view as friendly reminders of our fundamental Pristine Mind.

Even our habits at this third stage are friendly. Our positive habits may remain, but our negative habits are gone. If we have beliefs at this stage, they are positive beliefs that are in line with reality, not based on misjudgment and misperception; they are not narrow or prejudiced. If we have thoughts and emotions, they are positive and helpful—filled with great compassion, unconditional love, genuine appreciation, boundlessness, fulfillment, strength, self-confidence, and a mental and emotional sense of well-being. Everything in our mind is positive, because that is all that the environment of the mind at the third stage of awakening supports.

As we progress from the first to the second stage and from the second to the third stage of awakening, our experience of Pristine Mind expands more and more. The gap between mental events becomes wider and wider. This is why mental events lose their power and become less significant. The more we expand our experience of Pristine Mind, the more present and apparent that expansion becomes in each immediate moment. While mental events were predominant in the first and second stages, in this third stage of awakening, Pristine Mind is the predominant experience.

When we are at this stage, whether we are meditating or not meditating, whether we are awake or asleep, under all circumstances we are connected to the pristine, unpolluted, untainted mind as our predominant state of mind. Thoughts and emotions, mental events, are not central; instead, they are tangential, off to the sides of our awareness. Pristine qualities are at the center stage of our mind. Mental events are now like shooting stars occasionally darting across the sky. They pass by quickly.

Mipham Rinpoche says that at this third stage, our mind readily cooperates with us. If we want to remain in this pristine nature of our mind, we can do it easily. If we want to engage in something, it is easy to engage because our mind is no longer complicated. It becomes simple for us to deal with our mind. Our mind and our mental events listen and obey us. This is very different from the ego-dominated mind we started with.

Once we gain stability and familiarity with the true nature of our mind, our mind rests solidly and unwavering like a mountain. When our mind engages, it engages immediately and perfectly to do what we want it to do. Our mental events always obey us because we have full control over them. Everything we direct our mind to do, it does as we wish.

Wind Blowing through Empty Space

When our experience of the pristine state of mind becomes more stable and expansive, mental events are as harmless as wind blowing through empty space. However forcefully the wind blows through space, it cannot harm the space; it just passes through. Similarly, when our mind has become more spacious, when mental events do arise, they have almost no effect on us at all.

At this third stage, when everything that arises in our mind is a friend that supports our connection with Pristine Mind, we reflect on our experience during the first stage of awakening. We see such a huge difference that it creates a sense of incredible relief inside us. We feel amazing joy and happiness in our heart. We gain great confidence. This is another element of what a practitioner at the third stage of awakening can expect, Mipham Rinpoche says.

Mipham Rinpoche also says that once we have achieved victory over our mental events, we have conquered everything. We have no enemies or fears, and there is nothing left outside our pristine domain. No one and nothing can defeat us at this stage; we are victorious. We remain in a pristine state of mind under all circumstances, not just when we are meditating. Our Pristine Mind carries over into everything we do. When we are working, going anywhere, or doing anything, we operate from Pristine Mind. We have a profound and wonderful experience of our cloudless mind. Even when we do experience mental events, we have the most beautiful and positive mental events imaginable—mental events that embody our good heart. This is really what defines the third stage of awakening.

MASTERY OF OUR MIND

We have described how in the advanced stages of enlightenment our thoughts become allies and Pristine Mind takes the center stage of our experience. Mental events only happen off to the sides of our mind. They are merely peripheral. We have achieved mastery of our own mind.

Have you ever seen statues of the Buddha sitting in repose, still as a mountain? When we achieve mastery of our mind, we remain like a mountain, without wavering. This does not mean that enlightened beings spend all their time just staring into the distance without moving or even blinking. These statues instead represent the unwavering stability of the enlightened mind. In fact, while our mind rests in its natural state, our body may be in quick motion, doing any number of activities, and we can use our thoughts purposefully and effectively. Our mind can engage positively, calmly, and clearly; and we are more flexible, open, and dynamic. Our instincts are sharp. Positive emotions and thoughts arise more readily. We engage very consciously, productively, and properly. We have positive, beautiful, wonderful experiences, not the frustrations and disappointments we experienced when we were at the mercy of our mental events.

ENJOYING OUR MENTAL EVENTS

At this third stage, we can enjoy our remaining mental events, which are now under our full control. We can shape our mental events and increase and decrease them as it serves our objectives—objectives that are filled with love, compassion, joy, and appreciation for all beings.

When we are operating with an ordinary mind, as we do at the first stage of awakening, our mental events toy with us. They control every aspect of our life. We are like a marionette dangling on the puppeteer's strings. But once we have mastery of our own mind, then we can constructively and lovingly direct our own mental events. Our mental events are gentler and lighter; they lack the power they once had to drive our mind in the direction of chaos and self-defeating behaviors, because in this newly experienced environment our mind achieves stability.

We have the choice of our mental events and the direction of our mind. If we want to engage with mental events for constructive purposes of our own choosing, we can engage very positively and productively. If we choose to expand or dissolve any mental event, we can do that swiftly and without conflict. If we want our mind to be clear like a blue sky, we can also do that effortlessly. When we want to increase feelings like love, compassion, happiness, or enjoyment, we can choose that and it happens. We can increase mental events by focusing on them. We have complete authority and control over our mental events.

UNCONDITIONAL HAPPINESS

Guru Rinpoche Padmasambhava says:

> If you realize everything is your own perception,
> You experience unconditional happiness.
> If you remain free from ego and judgment,
> You experience natural happiness.
> If you are free from fixation within your natural mind,
> You experience boundless happiness.

When we have mastery over our mind, our happiness is unwavering and indestructible. Our mind becomes unmovable by conditions. Mental events cannot shake our mind at this third stage. Our happiness is no longer circumstantial, depending on particular conditions or happenings.

Once we have unconditional, enlightened happiness, whatever joys we have are stronger than they were in an ordinary state. The joy we experience when our mind is free from negative emotions is more powerful and vivid than when it is colored by negative emotions. When our mind is in an ordinary state, joy is not pure joy, happiness is not pure happiness, and love is not pure love, because everything is contaminated by ego and its misperception of the world in which it operates. Enlightened joy is not just ordinary pleasure; it is pure, stainless enjoyment arising from undistorted perception.

Everything becomes more pure in the third stage of awakening. We experience pure love, pure joy, pure happiness, and pure compassion. We have these pure experiences far more consistently. Under a hazy sky, we can see the sky but not with perfect clarity. But when all the haze clears away, there is nothing left but blue sky.

The more distorted our perceptions, the less pure our joy is. It's not natural or genuine. But without distortions, every experience we have is pure and authentic. The more pristine our mind becomes, the more pure, genuine, and real our life experiences are. Our experience is more powerful, more vivid, and more pristine.

Until we reach the second and third stages of awakening, our happiness is like a candle on a windy mountain peak. So many mental events keep blowing out the flame of our happiness. We constantly need to rekindle the flame. The instability of the candle flame is like the ordinary mind's attempts at happiness because there are so many mental winds blowing through the mind day and night. However, once the wind dies down, the candle burns continuously. In the same way, once all mental and emotional events subside, the flame of happiness burns steadily for longer and longer periods of time. We do not need to keep rekindling our happiness, because there are no gusts of mental and emotional wind to blow it out.

Compassion, love, joy, tranquillity, a sense of well-being, and all positive experiences and qualities become stable when the winds of mental and emotional events have calmed. All positive qualities then endure because there is no interference. The more pristine our mind, the more compassionate we are and the deeper our gratitude toward enlightened beings. We feel appreciation from the bottom of our hearts that enlightened beings like the Buddha and Guru Rinpoche Padmasambhava have gone before us and stood like beacons for this experience we now have. No one has to convince us to feel this appreciation. The experience of Pristine Mind itself elicits these positive emotions.

THE HEALTHY WAY OF ENJOYING SENSE PLEASURES

As a person progresses through the second and third stages of awakening, they are increasingly able to enjoy the pleasures of the senses in an authentic way.

When we think of sensual pleasures, we often think of sex as the primary example. It is true that sex can be one of the most intense forms of physical pleasure. But sensual pleasure is not just about sex. All of the ways that we enjoy the world through our senses, whether they are our favorite songs, delicious smells, or inspiring art, are sensual pleasures. Anything that causes joy or pleasure from the senses is a sensual pleasure. Through the stages of awakening, the more we awaken, the more we enjoy sensory experiences in an unpolluted way. When we encounter sensory experiences, we can experience them more fully, robustly, and authentically, without complications.

Once our mind is no longer controlled by mental distortions, then sensory experiences are no longer adulterated with bad habits, negative emotions, or negative thoughts. As a result, sensory experiences no longer make us suffer from the intensity of our reactions. The less distortion in our mind, the less turbulence sensory pleasures create.

To illustrate this, the pinnacle of sensual experience occurs in intimate relationships. When our mind is undistorted and pristine, an intimate relationship brings happiness, fulfillment, and extraordinary, blissful pleasure. But when our mind is filled with unhealthy habits, negative emotions, and ego, our love life becomes problematic. It is not, as some think, that relationships are inherently complicated. Instead, it is that our mind is complicated, making our relationships complicated. That is the true reason intimate relationships can seem so difficult. If our mind is in a keenly reactive mode, if our negative emotions are highly active, then the sensory experiences of an intimate relationship can quickly change from joy and ecstasy to conflict, anger, and disappointment. But if our mind more often remains in the equanimity and tranquillity of Pristine Mind, then the relationship is no longer problematic and its sensory experiences can be enjoyed for what they are—pure pleasure, uncomplicated by frustration, unrealistic expectations, or other negative mental events.

The Buddha's early teachings address attaining enlightenment through avoiding the temptation of all sensual pleasures, which were considered obstacles. The Buddha's later, advanced teachings, however, involve bringing all sensual pleasures onto the path to enlightenment and not avoiding them. The Buddha taught that these two different paths are for two different types of people. Some people, including those who become monks and nuns, attempt to avoid all sensual pleasures as a path to enlightenment. Most others do not want to give up sensory experiences in order to attain enlightenment. The Buddha taught that if you live in Pristine Mind, then you do not need to give up sensory pleasures to attain enlightenment.

Most of us are looking for pleasure through the five senses. We are listening to music, watching TV, gazing at scenery, holding hands, or eating delicious meals. Almost everybody seeks to enjoy those pleasures. They long to touch and be touched. They want to smell fragrances. Billions of dollars are spent on creating and providing sensory experiences.

The problem with sensory experiences is that when people have access to these sensory experiences, most do not know how to handle them. Every day they indulge themselves in sensory experience. There is music constantly playing everywhere in stores and restaurants. Everywhere people go, they expect or want to hear beautiful and pleasant sounds and see pretty sights. Since just about everybody wants to enjoy sensory experiences, then the admonishment "You should give up sensual pleasures" is unhelpful in most cases. So we need to learn how to incorporate sensory experiences into our spiritual path.

We do not need to abandon, avoid, or renounce sensory experiences in order to become enlightened. Instead, we can learn how to enjoy sensory experiences in a healthy way. We need to know the most authentic and genuine way to enjoy them. We can do this by following the teachings of the Buddha and Padmasambhava.

In his quest for freedom from suffering, the Buddha initially practiced self-denial and asceticism for years, renouncing all the sensory enjoyments that he had previously indulged in during his luxurious life as a prince. But in time the Buddha realized that the extreme of asceticism was not conducive to enlightenment. He also realized that to become fully awakened, the mind had to be liberated from all distortions, such as negative emotions. To accomplish this, it was necessary to work with the mind through meditation. This was a major turning point in the Buddha's path to enlightenment.

Through meditation, the Buddha's mind became completely pristine.

He then knew that enjoyments and sense pleasures were not required to be abandoned or rejected in order to become enlightened—they could be cooperative "ornaments" on the path to enlightenment. There is a famous story from the Buddhist scriptures about King Indrabhuti, who lived during the time of the Buddha. Each day the Buddha and his disciples would travel to different places where they would be hosted by various people for lunch, which was the Buddha's only meal of the day. Indrabhuti, who was very sincerely devoted to the Buddha and his teachings, invited the Buddha to lunch at his royal palace. The Buddha accepted the king's invitation. At this meeting, Indrabhuti requested the Buddha to please give him a teaching to transform his mind and attain enlightenment.

The Buddha began by testing the king to determine what teachings were most appropriate for him. The Buddha said, "If you want to attain enlightenment, you will first have to give up all your worldly attachments—your kingdom, your queens, your concubines, your life of luxury, and all the other pleasures of the senses that you enjoy. You will need to become a celibate monk. Then I will give you the teaching to attain enlightenment."

The king responded, "I fervently desire enlightenment, but I don't want an enlightenment without any pleasure—even if, by saying this, I am immediately turned into a fox! I would have no regrets. I don't want to attain enlightenment without pleasure, Gautama Buddha."

Then the Buddha knew what kind of teachings would most benefit the king. He gave him the teachings and methods for how to make sensory pleasures part of the path to enlightenment. As a result, Indrabhuti, his queens, his daughters, his ministers, and many others surrounding him, attained enlightenment in a single lifetime.

Many people think that following the teachings of the Buddha is only for monks and nuns, and requires giving up ordinary life and staying in monasteries or caves. But on the other side of the coin, you need to know about the yogi tradition. In the yogi tradition, you don't necessarily give up sensory pleasures and you can still attain enlightenment. You don't need to become a monk or a nun. If you have the right conditions and circumstances, receive the right teachings, and accomplish your meditation, then you can enjoy sensory pleasures as you continue to meditate and pursue enlightenment.

The Buddha gave us both of these paths—the tradition of monks and nuns, and the tradition of yogis and yoginis—as models to provide everyone with the best and most beautiful ways to handle mental, emotional, and sensual experiences, depending on people's different propensities. In both pathways, sensory pleasures can be successfully handled.

Many people suffer from the complications and turbulences of life because they don't know how to either avoid or transform their sensory pleasures. Without a proper way to handle sensory pleasures and our cravings for sensory experiences, we are at the mercy of the turbulent mental and emotional experiences that result. We can find ourselves drowning in uncontrolled passion, jealousy, conflict, fighting, and even, in extreme cases, killing. The Buddha's teachings are not religious principles; rather, he taught methods that we can all use as ways to handle our sensory experiences, and live fully on our journey to enlightenment.

When passions and sensual pleasures are mixed with ego and negative thoughts and emotions, it can be dangerous, poisonous, and even deadly. But there is nothing inherently wrong with passions and sensual pleasures; it all depends on the mental environment. If our mind is less influenced by the ego, if our mind is not filled with negative mental events, if we have a good heart, and if our mind is more pristine, then sensual pleasures become positive—not a hindrance to enlightenment, but a source of happiness and fulfillment.

To transform our sensory experiences into enlightened experiences, we need realization, meditation, and a good heart. We need a pristine and undistorted mind. All these things are the keys to enjoying sensory experiences. Enlightenment is not only the end of suffering; it is also the way to fully enjoy the world.

If there are no hindrances to our experience of the world, such as those created by the mental events we have been discussing, then when we listen to beautiful music, for example, it becomes part of our pristine experience. When our mind is pristine, then music is pristine because, ultimately, music is just pure sound. That sensory experience and our Pristine Mind are completely united and connected. They are unpolluted mental experiences—we can call them "pristine mental events."

With our ordinary mind, each form we see, each sound we hear, elicits judgments—whether resentment, attachment, or some other reaction that disturbs the flow of that union between our present awareness and our enjoyment of the world. But with enlightened mind, any sounds we hear, we hear in a very pure way. Enlightened beings can fully appreciate music, because they experience it in its pure state with absolutely no distortions, no preconceptions, and no disturbances.

The Dzogchen text *Symbol of Everlasting Victory* says, "All five sensory experiences become ornaments of your innate awareness." The more present and pristine our mind is, the more we enjoy each and every day in a very complete way. From the moment we wake up in the morning until we go to sleep at night, we experience a day full of contentment. Life's pleasurable experiences become ornaments of our pristine awareness.

The principles we have emphasized so far include the importance of connecting with enlightenment and the importance of having a good heart. Having a Pristine Mind includes enjoying the world, living properly and fully, and dying without confusion or fear. If we have a Pristine Mind, we will truly enjoy sensory experiences without creating hindrances. We feel perfectly connected to our friends and family and those around us. We feel connected to enlightenment. At the moment of our death, we have no fear or hesitation; we can remain in Pristine Mind. The goal is to have fewer restrictions—both worldly and spiritual—and more Pristine Mind. That is true spirituality.

25. The Fourth Stage of Awakening

The fourth stage of awakening is the highest stage, the absolutely perfect enlightened stage of awakening. This final awakening is the most precious, beautiful, and amazing stage attainable, the culmination of our journey into Pristine Mind.

Completely Perfect Enlightenment

In the previous stages of awakening, our mind became increasingly pristine as we progressed through the stages, but it was not completely perfect. Mipham Rinpoche says that in this fourth stage, whatever arises in the mind is enlightened awareness. There is no impurity, distortion, ego, or any kind of imperfection whatsoever. These things simply do not exist in this fourth stage. In fact, they *cannot* exist in this completely pristine environment. Everything that arises in the mind is pure and pristine at all times and in all ways. Everything is a function of enlightened awareness, the enlightened mind.

As ordinary people, we have difficulty even imagining the completely enlightened state because it is different from anything we have experienced. In a totally ordinary state of mind, we never get a taste of what enlightenment means. Once we reach the second or third stage of awakening, it is easier to accept and understand what the completely enlightened stage will be like.

Enlightenment is not just the perfection of our mental state, but the perfection of our entire experience. Every area of our life becomes completely perfect—our relationships, our experiences, our perceptions, everything. In enlightenment, everything is perfect. Everything becomes naturally and effortlessly perfect. This is why it is referred to as "completely perfect enlightenment."

You may ask how an enlightened person perceives the imperfect world, in which there is so much suffering, conflict, war, disease, and death. An enlightened person has the broadest and deepest possible view and always sees the big picture; such a person always responds to these circumstances with universal, all-pervasive, infinite compassion. So the mind of an enlightened person sees the suffering of beings at all times with uncompromising love and incomparably kind compassion, not with rejection, sadness, or any other negative feeling. This is the totally and naturally perfect mind of enlightenment. A person in ordinary mind, however, will perceive what happens and react in any number of ordinary ways, especially in negative ways, to situations that appear terrible. A person in ordinary mind might react compassionately to any particular situation. However, in ordinary mind, this compassion is limited to the particular situation and is colored by the ordinary mind's reactions, which are often distorted and complicated.

If your response to events is to feel how terrible everything is, then you have an ordinary mind-set. But if your response is compassion, then you have a positive mind-set. If you have boundless compassion and see the big picture at all times and under all circumstances, then you have the enlightened mind-set.

When our mind is polluted, it is because we are living in opposition to the nature of the universe. Conflict naturally arises for someone with such a mind because the polluted, distorted mind creates friction with the universe. Therefore, the universe feels like an enemy. But when our mind is perfectly in harmony with the nature of the universe, then the world cooperates with us. We are in harmony with it, and it is in harmony with us. It is our perfect ally. Harmonious experience develops freely between us and the entire universe around us. If our mind is perfect in its compatibility with the universe, the universe will cooperate with us. That is the nature of fully enlightened experience.

ENLIGHTENED MIND IS REAL MIND

Enlightenment is a measure of how well our mind is aligned with reality, undistorted by the ordinary mind, which misperceives on the basis of the desires and aversions that characterize our unenlightened attempts to find happiness and security. The more pristine our mind is, the more aligned we are with undistorted reality, the more we awaken. Enlightenment is the ultimately normal state of mind, and the ordinary mind is in fact, abnormal.

As we progress on the enlightenment journey, our mind becomes less fabricated, less contrived, and less distorted. We connect with the world more easily and straightforwardly because there are no barriers to doing so. People who have abnormal and distorted minds create walls and barriers that make it harder to connect with the world. It is harder for them to connect with friends and family as well as the rest of humanity. The more distorted the mind, the more barriers are created and the more difficult it is to relate to the world. In extreme cases, people can become completely isolated; since they are in such an abnormal state, they can't connect with anyone. This isolated existence is completely, utterly impossible at the fourth stage of awakening.

Some people, having an incomplete understanding about the nature of enlightenment and the process of attaining it, believe that the more enlightened one is, the harder it is for them to relate to or connect with the world, that they can only feel comfortable in isolation. Others view enlightenment as a deliberate disengagement from the world, not out of discomfort, but in rejection of all worldly activities. In both of these cases, it is thought that the mind of enlightenment is totally withdrawn from the world, enjoying its own separate experiences of bliss. However, one does not withdraw from the world in the enlightenment that arises from Pristine Mind—in fact, the opposite occurs. In Pristine Mind, one is aware of the world of ordinary mind but sees it clearly, without distortion, and acts skillfully in every situation. For someone ensnared in the abnormal, distorted state of mind, it can be very difficult and frustrating to function effectively. The more they are connected to the pursuits of the world of ordinary existence, the more toxic states of abnormal mind they have to contend with, and thus the more difficulty they have relating to the world. But when the mind knows the true reality of experience, without distortion, none of these problems exist.

Enlightenment lets us relate to the world easily and function in the world very effectively. Enlightened people no longer distort reality. They accept reality and, by doing so, can adapt to it effectively, without tension or ego-based reactions. For this reason, enlightened connections are real connections, enlightened compassion is real compassion, enlightened happiness is real happiness, enlightened mind is real mind, and enlightened reality is true reality.

Enlightenment means that every area of an enlightened being's inner experience is pristine, flawless, and authentic. All distortions in perception have disappeared. It is like the sun shining from behind dark clouds, brilliant and beautiful.

The more we progress along the stages of awakening, the more all of our abnormal states of mind gradually dissipate. We become mentally healthy and free from ego. Our mind is untouched by unhealthy misperceptions. When we reach the highest state of awakening, our mind is normal at every moment, no matter what we are doing or what may be happening.

UNDISTORTED PERCEPTION

Ordinary beings have distorted perception. Enlightened beings have undistorted perception. That is really the key difference. The more we progress along the stages of awakening, the less distorted our perception becomes. Our perception becomes more and more accurate and more in line with reality. Once we reach the highest level of awakening, then our perception is completely undistorted. Enlightened perception is perfectly undistorted perception. Nothing can distort it or pollute it.

When someone's perception is no longer distorted, any experiences they have are authentic, pristine, flawless, and perfectly in line with reality. There are no misperceptions. There is no self-consciousness or awkwardness because of all the misunderstandings that come from distorted perception. A person who does not have distorted perception does not have these reactions. The enlightened state of mind is completely different from the ordinary, confused state of mind. Enlightened perception is no longer distorted, and therefore the person's entire experience is totally healthy.

Pristine Mind practitioners have mastered their mind at the third stage of awakening. That means when thoughts or emotions arise, they have no effect. The mind of someone at the fourth stage is even more undistorted and unpolluted than at the second and third stages of awakening, because at the fourth stage of completely perfect enlightenment, there are no longer any negative tendencies, bad habits, or negative emotions. There is no attachment or aversion whatsoever. The fully enlightened person perceives the world perfectly accurately; they are seeing the truth.

The less distorted our mind, the more we see the world accurately, in an unfabricated way. We do not see it through distorted filters of beliefs or habits. We do not see it through any made-up state at all. We simply see pure reality as it is without characterization, manipulation, or judgment. When our mind is no longer distorted, when it is completely pristine, we see the world just as it really is.

Living in true reality, in Pristine Mind, is sometimes called "nonduality" because there is no separation between ourselves and everything else; there is no place where one can say our identity ends and the rest of the universe begins; there is no concept of "self" and "other." As a natural consequence of this, we are totally comfortable.

This is a progressive process. With each successive stage of awakening, primordial fear loses strength and fades away more and more. The more our mind resides in Pristine Mind, the less active primordial fear is.

Primordial fear cannot operate in the experience of nonduality, where we do not have an inflated or deflated ego that separates us from our world. In nonduality the world is simply continuous. There is no ego that we feel has to be protected from a world in opposition to it. Our awareness has expanded to encompass everything conceivable when we are fully, completely in Pristine Mind.

A HEALTHY SENSE OF SELF

In this fourth stage of awakening, when our Pristine Mind is completely awakened, the problems we talked about in the first part of this book—the distortions and pollutions of the ordinary mind—have completely disappeared because all mental events arose from losing touch with Pristine Mind. These all start from and depend on misperception. When misperception is no longer there, everything related to and caused by misperception dissolves. The more familiar we are with who we really are, our natural state, the healthier our sense of self will be.

As we journey through these four stages of awakening, as we become pristine, the environment of our mind is completely transformed and our sense of self becomes healthy, happy, and more flexible. Our mind becomes loose and relaxed. Our unhealthy senses of self, including low self-esteem and egocentricity, completely disappear. One of the most beautiful components of enlightenment is a perfectly healthy and pristine sense of self.

We do not need to avoid, overcome, or destroy our ego to be enlightened. Our sense of an ego is a misperception, so there is nothing real to overcome. Once we correctly perceive the true nature of reality, the problematic ego just vanishes like a burst bubble. We do not need a big hammer to make this happen. When our perception shifts, the ego just disappears.

The ego itself is circumstantial. With Pristine Mind prominent, instead of ego, a healthy sense of self arises. We feel a complete mental and emotional well-being that nothing else can match or disturb. This is enlightenment: a perfectly healthy state of mind. This is ultimately what we all want—to be totally fulfilled, incomparably comfortable, and completely harmonious with the universe. That is what the Buddha wants—for everyone to have this ultimate mental and emotional well-being.

No matter how famous we are, how much wealth we have, how high our status, or how beautiful or educated we are, these things do not give us a healthy sense of self. Realizing and residing within Pristine Mind gives us a pristine and totally healthy sense of self.

THE PASSING OF AN ENLIGHTENED BEING

When an enlightened being passes away, there is nothing to hold them down that makes their experience of death unpleasant. They do not resist the inevitability of death. Nothing can distract their buoyant Pristine Mind because there are no heavy mental events weighing down on their consciousness. They do not have any negative, unpleasant experience or fear. There is no terror of falling to some lower rebirth or hell-like realm, or passing into some unknown territory. They do not have such a strong attachment to the world that they cannot let go of it. Thus, when enlightened people pass, their mind effortlessly dissolves into the beautiful pristine state.

Those whose minds are pristine have pristine experience. They do not have polluted, distorted, or confused experience. The only dimension they can enter is a pristine dimension, such as a pure realm of enlightened beings.

And enlightened beings appear again in our world, out of their compassion to act as perfect guides for all others to attain enlightenment. To help others have Pristine Mind and become free from distortions, they reappear in many different dimensions, times, and places, and especially to human beings to help guide them to attain completely perfect enlightenment.

THE ONLY SAFE PLACE

Once we know about enlightenment and the process of Pristine Mind practice described in this book, then we know better how to relate to enlightenment. We don't need to treat it like some kind of foreign or exotic idea, or as if it is lifetimes away. We are able to relate to it and have an intimate, actual connection to enlightenment. This is really what we all want.

We are born into this world. Temporarily we connect with each other, but no matter how long the connection may last, ultimately we all go our separate ways. No one can know what will happen to them in this unpredictable, ever-changing world. Enlightenment is the most beautiful way to explain that there is something with ultimate meaning that we can know and achieve, to be truly happy. All other goals are just temporary and ultimately elusive.

Until complete enlightenment, everything is unstable and transitory. We cannot find anything material that will endure or make us happy no matter what. We want our mind to be pristine, consistently free from all entanglements and distortions, and unconditionally happy. That is what we want to experience. Only in that experience can we feel safe. There is no other safe place to go. The only truly safe place is Pristine Mind.

AUTHENTIC FAITH AND DEVOTION

True devotion—the appreciation we feel and express for enlightenment and the unconditional happiness it brings—is not based on blind faith. Devotion comes only through our own study and practice. The more we study, the more we practice meditation, and the more teachings we actually take into our hearts, the more inspired we will feel. Then we will experience a natural connection with enlightenment. This connection with enlightenment—not an unknowing trust in a mysterious "higher power"—is genuine faith.

The more we study and practice meditation and benefit from the meditation experience, the more we are drawn to manifestations of enlightenment, such as the Buddha and Guru Rinpoche Padmasambhava. We feel profound respect for them, our hearts open to receive their wisdom and compassion, and we are inspired to follow in their footsteps. That respect, that heart-opening experience, and that inspiration are also forms of devotion.

Genuine devotion and faith are not feelings that can be imposed by dogma or authoritarian decree. There isn't some kind of rule where we are told, "You must have faith and devotion." Faith and devotion come authentically from within. In our devoted state we really appreciate enlightenment and take refuge in it. We recognize it as our ultimate protection. These feelings occur naturally, without having to do anything to create them.

No one can tell us to fall in love. No one can say, "You must fall in love." The conditions need to be there for us to fall in love. To love someone, first we need to know that person. The more we spend time with that person, the more we see their qualities and characteristics, the more we appreciate and admire them. And then slowly through our interactions, through getting to know them more, we begin to fall in love with them and develop the intimate connection of love.

Devotion works exactly the same way. The more we study, listen to, and read the Buddha's teachings, the more we meditate and contemplate enlightened qualities, then the more a natural inspiration arises to connect with enlightenment. This connection to enlightenment naturally builds in our mind. We then truly respect, appreciate, and want to connect even more with enlightenment. Whether we are in a happy or a difficult time in our life, we admire and love enlightenment at all times. We always think and feel in our heart how special enlightenment is.

When we talk about faith and devotion, we are talking about building this type of connection with enlightenment. We sometimes hear the term "taking refuge" in Buddhist teachings. Once we have this type of faith and devotion, then we automatically take refuge in enlightenment. This devotion inspires us to practice meditation, and it inspires us to continue our practice in order to attain enlightenment. All these are the results of genuine, authentic devotion and faith.

As you progress in your meditation, you will find yourself thinking, "I really want enlightenment. I want it, I want it! Please give me a boundless mind right now, at this moment!" You will pursue your meditation with enthusiasm and determination. This is where your faith flowers and your devotion to the teachers of enlightenment blossoms.

All positive experiences will enter your life when you understand the teachings in this book and begin meditating. Something internally will click, and you will get it. When you see what was not seen before, everything opens and expands, and becomes crisp, clear, vivid, and brimming with wonder and freshness. All limitations dissolve and fall away. You will witness a tremendous process of growth in your appreciation of enlightenment.

This is my wish for you. Connect with Pristine Mind. Admire Pristine Mind, and rejoice in it.

HOMAGE TO GURU RINPOCHE
PADMASAMBHAVA

AFTER MANY YEARS of study, practice, contemplation, and meditation, thanks to the wisdom teachings of Guru Rinpoche Padmasambhava, this book has now been completed. This work has been a tremendous benefit to myself and others. In heartfelt gratitude and devotion for Guru Rinpoche Padmasambhava, these words appeared in my mind.

O Guru Rinpoche Padmasambhava,
I treasure your enlightened stainless awareness mind.
I am grateful for your boundless compassion.
I trust your majestic clear wisdom.
You are the embodiment of all enlightened ones.
You pour down tremendous love and compassionate teachings to
    all beings.
You care for all beings limitlessly.
Your enlightened speech is clear, pristine, vast, and profound.
It cools and heals the suffering and unhappiness of every being.
I am so moved by your boundless love and Pristine Mind teachings;
I cannot describe the immeasurable benefits for myself and others.
My gratitude rises from the bottom of my heart.
Without your wisdom and compassion, I cannot imagine
What I would do, what I would be.
O precious master Guru Rinpoche Padmasambhava,
Please help me to realize my mind is innately pristine.
Please help me to realize my mental events are just mental events.
Please help me to realize my mental events are illusions.
Please help me to completely awaken my Pristine Mind.

Please always pour down the nectar of your compassion and
   wisdom teachings
Until all beings' unhappiness and suffering end.
May all beings' minds become pristine and flawless.
May all beings attain completely perfect enlightenment.
Until then, please hold all beings with your infinite love and
   compassion.
OM AH HUNG BENZAR GURU PEMA SIDDHI HUNG

ACKNOWLEDGMENTS

I WOULD LIKE TO express my heartfelt gratitude to all the people who have helped to bring this book to life. Thank you from the bottom of my heart.

In particular, I thank Josh Godine for his tireless support over many years, including his faithful recording and transcribing of all the talks and teachings that form the foundation for this book. Many thanks to Heather Simon for her astute perception, assisting me in assembling and organizing these transcriptions into a coherent structure. To Bryant Welch, my thanks for his editorial skill in giving direction and momentum to the text. Thanks to Chuck Goldman, who worked with me for many months of rewrites, "deep cleaning" and polishing the text for tone, texture, and meaning. Thanks also to Maura Ginty for helping me translate the beautiful quotes in the book from Tibetan to English. And to Susan Pate, my thanks for her expert assistance in the design of the cover.

At Shambhala Publications, my gratitude to its dedicated staff, including John Golebiewski, for shepherding this book through the publication process, to Hazel Bercholz, for her skillful guidance in the design process, and especially to its president, Nikko Odiseos, for his unwavering faith in the ultimate success of this project. I also thank my editor Kendra Crossen Burroughs for her knowledge, advice, and stimulating commentary on successive drafts.

My heartfelt appreciation to the Board of Directors and everyone else involved in Pristine Mind Foundation for their support in so many ways and for their sincere dedication to our work. And finally, but so importantly, I am grateful to all my students, particularly those who helped with this book, for their open-mindedness, their enthusiasm, their thought-provoking questions, and their helpful suggestions.

About the Author

ORGYEN CHOWANG RINPOCHE is a meditation master in the Dzogchen lineage of the Buddhist tradition with a particular passion for presenting these teachings in a practical and experiential way for a modern audience. He studied for nine years with his teacher, Jigme Phuntsok Rinpoche, one of the greatest Dzogchen masters of the twentieth century. After completing his studies and receiving the *khenpo* degree, the highest degree of Buddhist study and practice, he spent several years teaching lamas, monks, and Western students at Ka-Nying Shedrub Ling, a large monastery in Nepal. During that time, he received additional advanced instructions from the renowned teachers Tulku Urgyen Rinpoche and Thinley Norbu Rinpoche.

Since 1995, Rinpoche has lived in the United States. He resides in the San Francisco Bay Area, where he is the founder and spiritual director of Pristine Mind Foundation. He conducts retreats and offers teachings throughout the United States and around the world, for a broad range of audiences, including business and technology professionals, parents, children, health-care providers, psychologists, spiritual seekers, and yoga practitioners. His teachings are also available online through live streams and recordings.

For information about studying with Rinpoche, including his schedule of teachings, please visit pristinemind.org.

About Pristine Mind Foundation

Pristine Mind Foundation, a nonprofit organization founded by Orgyen Chowang Rinpoche, is dedicated to helping people live fully, die fearlessly, and transform every area of their lives. The vision of Pristine Mind Foundation is for everyone to experience their Pristine Mind, and thus attain unconditional happiness. Through classes, retreats, audio and video recordings, translations, publications, online programs, and specialized training, the Foundation presents Pristine Mind meditation and other enlightened teachings in a way that is easily understood and directly experienced.

To learn more about Pristine Mind Foundation and Orgyen Chowang Rinpoche's activities, or to make a contribution to support this work and help preserve these teachings for future generations, please visit pristine mind.org.

PRISTINE MIND
FOUNDATION